DEADLY ASSOCIATES

by

Emma Seifert, Joe Seifert, and Nick Seifert

with

Matthias McCarn

Published by Chicago Scriptor LLC
ISBN# 978-0-692-98379-9

Cover Design by Octane Rich Media

Contents

Acknowledgments

(From the Seifert Family)

We would like to thank our families then and now for their continued love and support going through this terrible event.

Thank you to all the people who were willing to come forward after so many years and testify to the events of 9/27/1974.

Thank you to all government and law enforcement who never gave up believing that this murder and many others would finally get their day in court.

And a special "thanks" to Mitch Mars for his belief in this case. You will always be remembered with gratitude and respect.

Acknowledgments

(From Matthias McCarn)

Thank you to the Seifert family for your faith in my ability to tell your story. It has been an honor to work with you on this project and to get to know you on such a personal level. While this project comes to a close, I look forward to our continued friendship.

Thank you to my wife, who for several years, put up with me being locked in our study all hours of the nights and weekends writing, researching, and diving into a genre from which many people would want to run. I promised to keep our marriage interesting and being a part of this story certainly lived up to that!

Thank you to my two most influential university professors who generously took the time to review this manuscript. You both changed my life, and I will always treasure the experience in your classrooms.

Thank you to my family for your patience all those years while I was away, buried in work and school. And thank you to my uncle: without your generous support at such a critical point, my education would have stalled, and potentially stopped altogether. I will never forget that.

Dedications

This book is dedicated to Daniel R. Seifert.

Rest in Peace.

DEADLY ASSOCIATES

A Story of Murder and Survival

CHAPTER 1

Murder

Everyone has a dark side. A side that leans toward power and the fast lane, and causes a man to seek entry into a world that exists invisibly alongside the everyday; a world that average people glimpse on their TVs and in movies, on the news and in newspapers, but never experience. While most people will never touch upon it, even more don't realize just how close it is to everyday life.

Chicago has always been a cradle for this parallel world. Corruption, violence, payoffs, and Mob enforcers have, at times, seemed to be business as usual for the Second City. Known for its population of hard-working families, Chicago is also a city with a history of hard-working criminals. Empires have been built and destroyed around the intersection of power, corruption, and politics long before Al Capone ruled its streets in the early 20th century. But as Chicago matured, so did its criminals and their activities.

By the 1930s, Capone's control over the city had grown to levels never before imagined, and his corrupt influence lurked beneath all aspects of everyday society. Through that control, he reaped vast rewards of wealth, power, and influence, and formed an unstoppable syndicate that had mastered the development of lethal criminal minds; some of which still extend into the present day. And in early 1970s Chicago, Danny and Emma Seifert found themselves immersed in this underworld; linked to mobsters with direct lineages to Capone. Like so many others, they found that they couldn't escape its dangerous pull.

September 27, 1974 started out as a seemingly normal autumn day in the suburbs of Chicago for the Seiferts. About a year prior, they had opened their own fiberglass company, Plasti-Matic Products, in Bensenville, Illinois. They lived comfortably in a modest townhouse only a few minutes from their business in the shadow of O'Hare International Airport. On the surface, little would hint to differences between their family and the typical, middle-class neighbors who surrounded them. Emma, mid-twenties, was attractive and intelligent. She dressed fashionably for the 1970s and her blonde hair was always meticulously styled. Danny however, was more of an enigma. He was 29 years old, cocky, and tough. He wore a goatee and had dark hair that was combed back hipster style, which made him appear somehow misplaced for that time. But it was his eyes that hinted to the truth. They were calculating, intense, and echoed the soul of a man whose drive for success had moved beyond the point of possessive. For Danny, that drive had reached a level of destructiveness.

That morning, Danny drank his coffee, smoked his usual morning cigarette, and read the paper while Emma prepared breakfast for her family. Their son Joe, four years old at the time, was already taking after his father; not only in appearance but also in the form of mischievousness, and played sick to keep from having to go to day care. Joe's older step-brother, Nick, and step-sister, Kathy, siblings from Danny's previous marriage finished their breakfast and began to leave for school while Danny got ready to load the car and Emma gathered Joe's toys. Being a Friday, they had decided to bring Joe with them to their factory rather than to find a babysitter on such short notice—a decision that would come to haunt Joe, yet probably saved Emma's life.

As Danny started to walk through the front door, struggling with a vacuum cleaner they were bringing with them that day, Emma observed him unconsciously feel for the handgun tucked into his waistband before stepping outside. She thought to herself, "Only a few more weeks 'til the trial, and we can get past all of this."

Emma had reached a breaking point and wanted to get away from everything and everyone—except her children. The power and excitement that she and Danny experienced in the early days had long ago given way to fear and trepidation. She had, at times, even considered leaving Danny once the trial was over. She felt he had changed, especially over the last six months and she was afraid that he would never again be the man whom she had married. She was also increasingly concerned for the safety of their children. Through the glass of the front door, she could see Danny placing the vacuum cleaner into the trunk of their car, right next to a 12-gauge shotgun that he always carried with him. She brushed aside her feelings, took Joe's small hand in her own and stepped outside into the cool morning air to join her husband.

For the Seiferts, normalcy was non-existent. Things that the average person might take for granted were practically fairy tales to this troubled family. The children were not allowed to sleep over at their friends' houses, and friends were not allowed to spend time at the Seiferts' home. This was not only to protect Danny and Emma's own children, but also to protect their children's innocent friends. Emma had been taught by Danny how to shoot a gun so that she would be able to defend herself and their family if it ever came to that point. The children had been strictly taught not to touch their father's guns, which at times, would be laid openly on a coffee table

14

or the kitchen counter. For months, upon returning home from work, Danny would spend hours pacing and looking out the windows and repeatedly checking the doors to make sure they were locked. Most evenings, he would eventually fall asleep in his easy chair, exhausted, holding a loaded .45 in one hand and a glass of whiskey in the other. All of this was not simply out of paranoia as it would seem to most ordinary people. For Danny, it was out of necessity.

The Seiferts knew that Danny was in danger since he had agreed to cooperate with a federal investigation that focused on his former business partners, some of the top mobsters in Chicago. These partners included Felix "Milwaukee Phil" Alderisio, Mob leader from 1969 – 1971[1]; alleged Mob Capo Joey "the Clown" Lombardo, known for his grip on Las Vegas and close dealings with famed Mob hit man Tony "the Ant" Spilotro; and Irwin Weiner, a bail-bondsman and known Mob financier with ties to Jimmy Hoffa and infamous assassin Jack Ruby—ties that would land Weiner in front of the JFK Subcommittee hearing in 1978[2] to testify about his possible links to the Kennedy assassination. And these former

---

[1] Organized Crime and Political Corruption
http://www.ipsn.org/a century of chicago mob bosses.htm

[2] JFK Subcommittee Hearing, Executive Session, House of
   Representatives, May, 18, 1978.

partners were far from pleased with Seifert's cooperation with the Feds.

By agreeing to testify, Danny Seifert had become a key witness in a massive federal investigation into the Mob's infamous involvement with the Teamsters Central States Pension Funds. Danny's former business partners were the targets of that investigation, and he knew all. This knowledge put him in the lethal position of being threatened by the Chicago Mob to not talk, and being threatened by the Feds with hard time for his dealings with the Mob. He found out quickly that there was nowhere for him to turn and absolutely no one to trust. Danny placed the blame of his predicament squarely on his partners, whom he felt destroyed not only his company by taking their illegal activities to such a blatant level, but also destroyed his future and the future of his family. To Seifert, the Mob had taken things too far.

But no one at the time realized to what extent Danny's former associates were prepared to go to keep him quiet. It is also unclear and unanswered why Danny had apparently refused or was not offered any witness protection. He had kept much of the information about the case from Emma in order to protect her and their family. As a result, she didn't know the true depth of corruption to which Danny had been exposed; and more importantly, just how much he knew about that corruption. She had no idea that Danny's former partners were being accused of siphoning millions from the Teamsters and laundering that money through his former company,

International Fiberglass, in the form of fraudulent loans. Danny's hand was forced and his ultimate decision to cooperate with the Feds made him a direct threat to the Chicago Mob, and its leaders. As far as the Mob was concerned, there was no other solution—Danny had to be eliminated.

As Danny and Emma made the short drive to their fiberglass factory that morning, they didn't notice spotters along their route watching their approach. Observers in cars sitting in restaurant parking lots watched them pass by. A man in a seemingly broken down car on the side of the road radioed ahead with their progress. The gangsters used Mob "work" cars that incorporated flip-down fake license plates, switches to disable brake lights, hidden gun compartments, untraceable registrations, and police radios to know the locations of all the cops within the intended area. When a hit was ordered within the Chicago Mob, it was orchestrated with an almost military level of efficiency and planning. There were rarely loose ends.

During a 2008 interview for this book, veteran news reporter John "Bulldog" Drummond discusses the Mob's level of planning with regard to Seifert and other hits:

"Any time you have an organized crime case where there's a murder with organized crime involved, [...] the people involved are considered professionals. It's not a crime of passion; it just doesn't happen. It's usually thought out just like a minor military operation."

Emma remembers that Joe played with his cars in the back seat while Danny was unusually quiet that day. As they reached the small office complex where their factory was located, Danny pulled into the entrance rather than enter as he usually did through the parking lot's exit. This would seem normal to most people, but Danny always entered through the exit, which allowed full view of the back door into the factory, giving them a chance to see if someone had broken in during the night; and more importantly, if someone could still be inside.

When she questioned him on this point, she recalls, "He didn't answer and just pulled up to our parking spot near the front door." She thought he was just consumed with the upcoming trial and let it go. She exited the car and grabbed Joe out of the back seat. Danny opened the trunk, and then walked with Emma to the front door. As they opened the office door, nothing seemed out of place. They entered with Joe and she told Danny that she'd start making the coffee, then watched him go back outside to the car to grab the vacuum cleaner.

As Emma began to fill the coffee pot with water, two masked gunmen burst through the rear door that led to the factory section of their office. Emma screamed. The men were dressed in dark clothes and wore ski masks. But the masks had no eyeholes; only thin, cut slits so that no one who would look at the men could clearly see their eyes. Joe stood in shock staring at the fierce men as they stormed into the office. Emma noticed that one of the gunmen was carrying a thick briefcase, which he set on the floor as he approached her.

"Don't scream," he told her. "We're just going to rob you; we aren't going to hurt you."

She began to reply that they had no money in the office, when the other gunman pushed her to the floor. Just as he demanded, "Where is that SOB," Danny stepped unknowingly back inside the office. He had never heard the men enter and was immediately jumped by one of the gunman. Danny started to fight furiously, as a third gunman ran into the building from outside and joined in the fight. One of them managed to pull Danny's gun from his waistband rendering him helpless as they viciously beat him with their pistols.

Joe witnessed the men beating his father and recalls, "My memory of the scene is only black and white. I don't remember any sound at all. I was terrified, frozen, staring at these men beating my father. I do remember the dark red blood, which is the only thing that seemed to be in color. I was so young, I just wanted them to stop and I wanted to go home. I wanted everything to go back to normal. I was just a little kid at the time and I couldn't understand what was happening."

In the confusion of the fight, Emma moved Joe out of the way and scrambled for her desk where she kept a loaded .38 caliber pistol, but found that the drawer was locked. The second gunman saw Emma at the desk and immediately grabbed her and Joe and began to push them both at gunpoint into the bathroom.

She trembled with fear and anger. She thought she recognized the man to be Danny's former partner, Joey "the Clown" Lombardo, because of how he moved and his mannerisms.

"Lombardo had been a boxer and had a very unique characteristic to his movements," Emma would later tell the investigators when she was asked about her suspicion.

As they were being pushed into the bathroom, she could hear that the other two gunmen continued to beat Danny. She and Joe then heard a single gunshot. Danny had been shot in the cheek and was now bleeding profusely from the beatings.

By this time, Danny was already critically hurt and his son Joe, rather than crying louder, became withdrawn and grew strangely silent. All Emma could do was focus on the man pressing the gun to her head as sounds of the violent struggle pierced the small office. For a moment, time seemed to stand still. Then, as abruptly as everything started, sounds of the struggle ceased. Their captor told Emma not to move and slowly backed out of the bathroom into the front area, grabbing the briefcase from the floor. The office then fell silent except for her young son's quiet sobs.

Emma's heart pounded. She felt sick as she feared desperately for her husband's life. Within seconds, she gathered herself and found the courage to go out into the front office space, which was now empty.

"I thought that Danny might have escaped," she recalls. "Signs of the struggle were everywhere and I saw blood all over the walls in the entry way."

She tried calling the police but the lines were busy. She then ran to the desk, unlocked it, grabbed her gun from the drawer and ran to the front door. She slowly began to push it open to look outside for Danny.

"I saw him running through the parking lot being followed by two men; one carried a pistol, and further back another was holding a sawed-off shotgun."

To this day, she clearly remembers the glint of the shotgun standing out in the grey light of that cloudy morning, noting that it was nickel-plated. This seemingly small point only emphasizes the brazenness these men had. They knew they were going to get away with this. The Mob controlled Chicago and many of the suburbs at that time, and because of its reputed grip on the local police and some politicians, it didn't have to be discreet. With Seifert, the Mob wanted to make a point.

"The gunman holding the shotgun happened to see me open the front door and turned and pointed the gun toward me, smiling. I frantically closed the door and locked it, and then tried again to call the police. I finally got through and pleaded desperately for help. I then called my sister Judy. I began to cry to her, 'They got him. They got him.'"

Outside, a critically wounded Danny was bleeding heavily, but somehow found the strength to sprint into another warehouse. A fourth gunman, also with a shotgun, had been waiting outside and picked up the chase with his partners. Danny was helpless against the odds. He ran through an adjacent warehouse and out a side door with several gangsters in close pursuit. As he tried to cross the parking lot, a gunman with a pistol fired and hit Danny in the knee. He stumbled and fell beneath a large tree. A witness who had just arrived at work that morning then stared in horror as another gunman, in broad daylight, calmly walked up to Danny who was still trying to crawl away, and fired once with a shotgun to the back of Seifert's head. The killers then immediately fled in three getaway cars.

By now, Emma had returned to the front door and didn't see anyone nearby. She cautiously unlocked it and stepped outside holding onto Joe with one hand while holding her pistol in the other. She began to frantically look around the parking lot as witnesses started to slowly come out of the nearby offices in response to all of the commotion. Emma started to break down and began to scream repeatedly to everyone around, "They killed my husband! They shot my husband!"

After the police arrived, they approached Emma and carefully took the gun from her hand. Judy arrived minutes later and found a confused and scared Joe clinging tightly to his mother. She tried to comfort the young boy as best as she could and together, she and Emma gently put Joe in the back seat of her car. But Joe remained silent and still wouldn't talk. Judy and Emma then went to speak briefly to the police and demanded to pick up her other children before going through any investigation. In the back seat, Joe looked around at the chaotic scene of police and reporters and then saw his father's lifeless body lying face down in the grass, still uncovered, crumpled underneath a large tree. It would be the last memory Joe would ever have of his father.

CHAPTER 2

Aftermath

The morning of Danny's murder, officers had begun to arrive within several minutes after other people in the office complex had called the police. By then, Emma was hysterical and the police wanted to get her away from the scene and question her on the situation. She refused; demanding that she pick up Danny's other children before she would speak to anyone. Emma was terrified that something might have happened to Nick and Kathy, and suddenly remembered something strange from the previous day.

"A young girl had called asking about what time they needed to be at school, but Kathy didn't know her," Emma recalls.

Initially troubled by the call, Emma contacted the school and discovered that no one was enrolled with the name given by the caller, "Joanne Schaffer."[3]

"Back then, we couldn't imagine that the Mob, as devious as they were, would use a child to do their work. They were gangsters, but they still had a strict code to follow."

Since it was a young girl who called, Emma and Danny dismissed the incident as coincidence rather than something more sinister, and felt it was safe to let them go to school. She now feared that decision had been a tragic mistake.

Emma's sister Judy arrived just moments after the police. When describing the scene, Judy remembers, "The police tried to stop me as I ran up, but I pushed right through them and ran to Emma. I was annoyed with the cops because they kept trying to ask Emma all these questions, but my first concern was the safety of her and Joe."

Together, she and Emma adamantly told the police that they would only talk after they picked up the other children to make sure they were safe. There was no negotiation on this. The police finally gave in and escorted them to the school to pick up Nick and Kathy who, thankfully, were found to be unharmed.

---

[3] FBI Interview, Emma Seifert, October 8, 1974.
http://blogs.suntimes.com/mob/2009/01/emma_seifert_fbi_interview.html

By this time, police investigators and news crews started appearing at the scene. Detectives had discovered a pair of handcuffs on the ground outside of Seifert's office. It would later be determined that the killers had intended to capture and torture Danny and possibly even Emma before eventually killing him. Yet because of how hard he fought, he was able to escape the office and lead the men away from his wife and child. In addition, the fact that his son Joe happened to be there that day most likely changed the plans of the killers, forcing them to leave Emma alone. Rarely did the Mob ever kill a woman, even the wife of an intended victim. But they certainly never crossed the line and took out a child; especially that was one so young and even more so while the mother was right there next to him.

As detectives began to examine Danny's body, they saw how badly he had been beaten and were amazed that he had found the strength to run. The coroner's report states; "multiple lacerations to the skull caused by blows from a blunt object (gun butt)." The examiner determined that these blows were of a "lethal potential" even before Danny had been shot.

Before the days of cell phones and the Internet, reporters, like the mobsters, would usually monitor the police scanners for any activity. That morning when the calls came in about the shooting, crews immediately left for the scene. CBS News reporter John Drummond's crew was the first to arrive at Seifert's factory.

"We came to the scene and we didn't know who Danny Seifert was, […] but the man had clearly been shot," Drummond recalls. "It had all the earmarks of an Outfit hit. And right away we knew that this was quite a story."

After he began talking to investigators and witnesses on the scene, the veteran reporter started to put the pieces together.

"We found out soon after that Seifert was a key government witness. That changed the whole tenor of the thing. It was obviously a big, big story. But a murder in broad daylight is very rare. And when a man is pursued through the [factory] by the killers, who obviously were very determined to kill him […] with his wife and child on board, it was very, very unusual to say the least."

Witnesses on the scene began to recount what happened to the investigators and the reporters, and the story quickly spread to the local TV stations.

After picking the children up from school, Emma then brought the children to her parent's house in nearby Melrose Park, Illinois, where her family was already gathering to support her. She recalls, "My mother became hysterical when I told her what happened, while Nick, Joe, and Kathy were in the next room. I was upset because I knew that they had heard their grandmother's reaction, which meant I had to tell them what happened to their father right away."

At this time, Emma didn't tell the children that Danny had been murdered; only that he had been killed in an accident. She wanted to keep that knowledge from them not only to prevent them from being afraid, but also because the children knew the people, whom she suspected, were involved. The men responsible for Danny's murder were considered uncles by the children, and they had many times taken the children to the circus, ball games, or even just out for a hamburger. Joe had even been named after Lombardo; the very person Emma knew deep down was directly responsible for her husband's murder. They were far too young to be able to handle the truth, let alone begin to understand the scope of what had really happened to their father.

Judy then went back to check on the scene, while Emma, now joined by her other sister Virginia and Danny's two brothers, Tom and Bob, followed the police back to the station so she could give an official report. By then, there were reporters all over the scene at the Bensenville police station and they began to swarm around a shaken Emma as she arrived. Judy left the factory and then rushed to the police station and remembers "pushing the asshole reporters out of my way," as she entered the station to find her sister.

To Emma, all of this is a blur. She recalls bits and pieces, but mostly remembers the fear she had for her children; afraid that these men might still come after her, her children, or even her family. Because of that fear, she was extremely cautious on what information she gave to the police. She didn't know whom she could trust or who was connected to the Mob. Initially, she wouldn't even name anyone she thought was connected to the murder. "I don't believe I would want to state that right now," is all she would repeatedly say to the Detective in charge of the investigation when asked about possible suspects or individuals that could be responsible for her husband's murder.

However, since the police already had a complaint on file from December 13, 1972[4], regarding "indirect threats upon life" from Joey Lombardo to Danny, she eventually decided to go ahead and mention Lombardo's name. The complaint clearly pointed out Lombardo and Weiner's prior involvement with Danny, including the intimidation tactics they had begun to use against him. Emma realized it would only be a matter of time until the police found that report, and decided to go ahead and mention Lombardo and why she thought she recognized him.

Finally, after spending several hours in the interview room, Emma, Judy, Virginia, and Danny's brothers left the police station to return home. As they exited the police station, reporters immediately surrounded the family, screaming harsh questions at them.

---

[4] Police Report. Bensenville, Illinois, December 13, 1972.

"Do you know who killed your husband?" several reporters yelled out. Another screamed directly to Emma, "Did you know your husband was in the Mob?"

Through the chaos of the screaming reporters, two stood out to Emma. The first was John Drummond. "He treated us with respect, and was the only one that was a gentleman. Because of that, to this day, he is the only reporter that I will interact with and has become a friend to our family."

Drummond recalls of that day, "Consider what had happened to Emma Seifert. Her husband had been gunned down in broad daylight. So, it was a very traumatic thing for her. We tried to treat her with some respect, not shouting questions at her or anything like that. There was very little that she could say. Number one, the authorities didn't want her to talk about it very much; and number two, consider the situation she was under. She obviously was traumatized about the situation. We tried to treat her like a lady."

But Emma also remembers one reporter in particular who didn't seem to fit with the others.

"I remember that he had an evil look on his face," she recalls of the man. "He was a big guy, dark hair, glasses—and he fired a nasty question at me, which I honestly can't recall now. I just remember that something about the guy didn't seem right to me. And when we pushed through the crowd near him, I heard someone close by say to us in a very soft tone, almost a whisper, 'He got what he deserved.' Whether this guy said it or not, I don't know, but it came from that direction and seemed more like it was spoken to me, rather than called out to us in general."

After the family left the police station, they went straight to the bank and drained all accounts of money. Danny always kept a large amount of cash in their personal checking account to cover business expenses. Since Emma had no idea what the result would be of any police or FBI investigations, she needed to make sure that all possible funds were going to be available for her and her children to survive.

Once the money was secured, they returned to her parent's house. Family members were concerned because Joe was in shock and still wouldn't talk. Emma remembers walking into the front room and seeing that someone had turned on the TV. She went over and ripped the plug out of the receptacle so that the kids wouldn't see the news.

"At the time, I was trying to protect them from everything I could," she recalls. "I certainly didn't want them to see or hear about their father's murder on the TV. I still hadn't had the time to react to everything because I was so consumed with protecting them. I was also very concerned for Joe; not only because of what he saw, but also because he wasn't talking."

Danny's two brothers demanded that Emma hand over Danny's guns so they could take revenge, but she would have none of it. Not because she didn't want some sort of justice done to the men who killed her husband, but as she would later write in a journal, "Danny's brothers had their own guns and certainly didn't need Danny's. But, there was already too much sorrow; we didn't need anymore. My children didn't need anymore. They needed security, which only my family could provide, and not with guns or more shooting."

The future of her children would become the sole motivation that enabled Emma to continue to live day-to-day; to survive as a widow and mother in a violent and uncertain time.

"I desperately feared for the children's safety, and didn't want any more bloodshed," Emma recalls. "I was sick of the guns. Danny had guns all over the house and in the office, and they didn't help. He kept a shotgun and three handguns in the office, and a rifle and three handguns in the house at all times. There was a gun always within reach and he used to take me shooting at Bells Gun Range in Franklin Park, so that I knew how to fire a handgun. But they still killed him. They still got to him. Now, my first priority was the safety of the children. Nothing would get in the way of that."

After taking care of everything she needed to do at her parent's house, Emma then left to go and get clothes and belongings for the children from their home. She and her sister walked into the Seifert home now haunted with memories of her husband and their family. Upon looking for various things to bring back to her parent's house, they discovered an unsigned life insurance policy valued at one million dollars sitting on top of the refrigerator.

"Danny and I had met with an insurance agent to take out a life insurance policy only a few days before, but he hadn't signed it yet," Emma remembers.

Financially speaking, she then realized just how difficult the survival situation for her and her family would be. A distraught Emma then picked out items that she felt the children would need, gathered her own belongings, and then prepared to return to her parent's home that evening. She walked by the couch and her mind back-flashed to a premonition of Danny's death that she had a couple weeks prior to this terrible morning.

"I had come down the stairs and Danny was sleeping on the couch, positioned just like he would be in a coffin," she recalls. "At that moment, I had a gut feeling come over me that this situation would not end well for him. But it was one of those things you just dismiss as nerves and move on."

Only a few nights before the murder, Emma also had a dream about the events that were about to come. She recalls, "It was so bad that I forced myself to forget about it. I still think that somehow, if I had said something to him, things might have turned out differently; that I might have been able to change what had happened to him."

It had only been hours since the murder of Danny, yet Emma had already endured so much in such a short time. But for her and her children, this would only be the beginning. Upon returning to her parent's house and making sure the children were safe, she collapsed. Judy found her crying, inconsolable, and rocking back and forth on the floor.

Emma had her family, but deep down she knew that she was now alone. She had no idea whom she could trust, including police or federal investigators, or to whom besides her own family she could turn. She didn't know if Danny's killers would return for her, her children, or even her extended family members. In addition, she needed to figure out how to provide the essentials that she and her children would need to survive, since she now faced a future of raising three children by herself. She also knew that she would soon have to return to the factory where her husband was murdered and try, somehow, to make it all work. Emma would eventually come to discover that by killing Danny, the Mob would slowly and methodically torture her and her children for the rest of their lives.

CHAPTER 3

Twisted Roots

By the time Danny Seifert went into business with Irwin Weiner and Felix Alderisio, he knew that his new business partners were connected to the Mob. The aspects of danger, power, and the Mob lifestyle were exactly what drew him in deep. His mistake came in thinking he could control the partnership and leverage their powerful influence for his own self-interest. Danny had convinced himself and even Emma that he could walk the fine line of partnering with gangsters but not really becoming one himself: enjoying a life of being able to reap the criminal rewards and living a Mob lifestyle but not being involved with the crime personally. But, the seduction to which he had fallen prey would run far deeper than power or money. As his son Joe now says, "It's in our blood." To this day, the lure of the Mob lifestyle pulls at the Seifert family constantly.

For Danny, interacting with the Mob came easily. When he was born on April 28, 1945, his father Nicholas had already been connected to the Mob for years. He too, had experienced the pull and influence of money and power. Nicholas would use Mob money to secure bad real estate loans for people whom he and his associates knew wouldn't qualify for a reputable loan at a bank. These loans would be set up with a very high interest rate and once the people defaulted, which was inevitable, the Mob would then come in and take back the property no questions asked. Having made money on both the initial sale and the interest, they would then turn the repossessed property around to another unsuspecting or desperate buyer and repeat the lucrative process.

This practice, however unethical, was extremely lucrative for Nicholas. The business afforded his family the best things money could buy, including houses, cars, maids, personal drivers, and even horses. However, his dealings with the Mob, the full extent of which are not completely known to his surviving family members, would begin to catch up to him as Danny grew older.

What is known is that around late 1955, when Danny was ten years old, Nicholas was accused by the Feds of being involved in a murder. Because of the severity of the charges, he took his family and fled to California in 1956 until his Mob lawyers could smooth things over for him. Once his attorneys worked their magic, the Feds eventually dropped the case in 1958 allowing Nicholas to move his family back to Lincolnwood, Illinois, just outside of Chicago. But the case against him and the subsequent relocation had an adverse effect on Nicholas' business and family; and this would prove to be the catalyst of a steep downward spiral for the Seifert family.

By this time, the marriage between Nicholas and Danny's mother, Antoinette, had deteriorated. They fought bitterly. Nicholas openly had affairs and Antoinette had become a severe alcoholic due to her husband's neglect and his Mob lifestyle. For the children, it was already too late. They were forced to grow up too fast, and the boys especially had gotten the taste of easy money and influential power from their father--and they wanted more.

Danny was the youngest of four children, with an older sister and two older brothers. Tom, the oldest son, was in his early twenties when they moved to Lincolnwood, Illinois, and had already been forming his own connections with local gangsters. Danny and Bob, three years apart, still had time before forming their own connections, but watched their father and Tom closely and learned from them. Shortly after they moved, things would begin to change drastically for the Seifert family. Nicholas died of a heart attack in the bed of one of his mistresses, and less than one year later the IRS came in and seized all of the family's assets to cover the back taxes that Nicholas owed. In the blink of an eye, Danny had not only lost his father, but the Seifert family was now broke.

Antoinette would end up moving the family from the suburbs into Chicago in search of a new life. It is unclear if it was planned or not, but they ended up moving into a north-side Chicago neighborhood that happened to be home to several Mobsters, and their kids. These Mobsters' children were being groomed to be the next generation and future leaders of the Chicago Outfit. It was here that the brothers would form fateful friendships that would ultimately prove to be lethal for Danny. Not surprisingly, details of these friendships are vague. At the time of writing this book, Danny's oldest brother Tom, is in hiding and hasn't been seen by the family for years. Bob, the middle brother, refuses to this day to speak about his connections, "friends," or any specific details about his involvement, for fear of Mob retribution. Neither has used their real names for decades, but the rest of the family does know the basic elements of their stories.

A couple years after moving to Chicago, Bob was old enough to join the Army, while Tom stayed back in the neighborhood. Tom had made friends with some powerful people and he started to make a living by boosting trucks for the Mob. He and his associates would put the drivers on their payroll, which meant beating them up to make it look like a real robbery and giving them money not to talk. Once a driver got on the program, they found that they could make much more money giving up a load than doing their normal work.

For the more unwilling drivers, Tom and his associates would find other creative ways to "convince" them. Threats against a driver's family were usually all it took to secure the goods with little to no resistance offered in return.

After a few years of this activity, Tom was fully entrenched in his shady dealings and Bob returned home from the military. In need of work and armed with skills learned in the Army, Bob became connected with a local motorcycle club. Through them and his brother's connections, he too started working for the Mob. It is unclear exactly what aspect his "work" was with them, or even for how long he was involved. Yet in 1974, just weeks before Danny's murder, Lombardo would repeatedly call Bob, warning him that they needed to convince Danny not to talk, or else. Danny never paid any attention to the relayed messages. But Lombardo's warnings pointed directly to what the Mob viewed as Danny's transgressions. In the Chicago Outfit, blood is not thicker than gang loyalty. Danny's willingness to talk to the Feds sealed his fate as far as the Mob was concerned.

Interestingly, even though no connection was ever established between Bob and Lombardo in any investigation, in January of 2006, Joey "the Clown" Lombardo, the man now convicted of murdering Danny, was seen sitting in the alley behind Bob's house just days prior to getting arrested while sitting in another alley. When Bob's wife pointed out that Lombardo, who had been on the run for over nine months by that time was out back, Bob replied to her, "Let him rot."

Danny, as he grew older, would not forget what a big-time lifestyle that his father had; and more importantly, what he had lost. After the IRS took everything that the Seiferts owned, he survived as any street kid does—through hustling. Danny was always cocky and tough, and on the street he began to hone his skills. He became fast friends with a neighborhood kid named Warren Osborne. Together, the two spent their time together running scams and finding any way they could to make a buck.

But Danny was different than his friends from the streets. He was talented, extremely ambitious, and a natural entrepreneur. At just fifteen years of age, Danny started working with Warren on fiberglass. Warren worked at an auto garage doing fiberglass auto body repair and he brought Danny in to help and make some extra money. Danny learned quickly and found that he worked well with his hands. He also discovered that he enjoyed it.

The two did very well and started making good money repairing cars, boats, photography sinks, or anything else made with fiberglass that they could find to work on. When work was slow, they would also prowl around different boat harbors in the city to vandalize the fiberglass hulls on private boats. They would then return a day or two later, planting their business cards all over the harbor slips to get the lucrative business that they had just created for themselves.

When they still couldn't make enough to support their increasingly demanding lifestyle, they came up with the idea of scamming the owner of the auto garage they worked in. The two agreed to have Danny beat up Warren just enough to make it believable to the cops and then they would steal the cash and stage a fake robbery. After hiding the money and tying up Warren, Danny called the police and told them some black guys came in and roughed up Warren and took the cash. No one ever suspected anything, which was the green light for Danny and Warren to do this more than once. For months, the police were on the lookout for a couple of black guys with enough guts to go into the north side of Chicago where they would have stood out like sore thumbs. Danny and Warren got some extra spending money and the robbery cases, needless to say, went unsolved.

Danny worked with Warren out of that garage for a couple of years and during this time met a young woman named Barbara. Shortly after they met, Barbara became pregnant and in early 1962, when Danny was just 17, the two were married. Keeping to Danny's fast-track schedule for living, they had their first child together on May 9, 1962. Named after Danny's late father, Nick was born into a building lineage of corruption. However, now that he was married and had a child, things would begin to change for Danny. He realized that he needed more money and a more ambitious source of income, and direction. Danny and Warren would work together for another couple of years, but eventually they shut their business down in 1964, the year after Danny and Barbara would have a daughter, Kathy.

Danny wanted more than what he could make in a small business running out of a garage. He wanted the level of success that his father experienced and Danny saw a unique, lucrative opportunity to do so with fiberglass. He knew that the 1950s and 1960s had seen an increase in the production uses for fiberglass. Already used extensively for aircraft, fiberglass had found its way into auto and boat manufacturing and in 1953, Chevrolet partnered with Owens Corning and built the first ever production vehicle with a fiberglass body, the Corvette.

Danny knew that production use would only continue to increase and decided to form his own fiberglass business. However, he also knew that it needed to be built on a much larger scale than the type of work that he had done with his friend, Warren. Danny just needed the capital to take his business idea to the next level. It would turn out to be another of Danny's friends who would introduce him to someone who would not only offer up the funds for such a business, but would be a dark, influential force upon Danny and forever change the direction of his life.

CHAPTER 4

Sacrifice

Following the path of his own parents, by 1965 Danny's marriage to Barbara was already failing. The two were constantly having terrible fights and started going through a bitter separation and custody battle. After one particularly heated exchange, Danny followed Barbara to a Toys-R-Us store and while she was inside, proceeded to smash out all the windows of her car with a baseball bat, right in the middle of a busy parking lot.

By 1966 when he was only 21, Danny found himself separated with two kids. To support himself and his children until he could create his larger-scale company, he did side jobs wherever

43

he could, including some work with his friend Warren. At this time, like Danny, Warren was also married. But true to a hustler's lifestyle, he always had some amorous action on the side. Warren was dating a young woman named Sue, who happened to be the cousin of another young woman, Emma, who would eventually become Danny's second wife.

When she was just five years old, Emma's family had moved to Chicago from Winchester, Illinois, a small town about 250 miles south of Chicago. Like many small-town families, her father decided to pack up his family and head to a bigger city in the hopes of making more money and finding more opportunity for himself and his family. This change would result in unforeseen problems for Emma as she grew up, and the opportunities would be of a much darker nature than her father ever imagined for his small-town family.

Growing up, Emma had enjoyed a good childhood and was the youngest of five children. She was raised not far from where Danny was raised, but the two lived a world apart. She had good relationships with her parents and sisters, and to this day, her older sister Judy is someone she can always turn to for strength. In high school, Emma was ambitious and hardworking, but she was an average student who was more concerned with working and earning a living than going to college. She spent her senior year of high school splitting her school days in a work program, which taught her office skills for class credit and allowed her to earn some extra money. She grew close to her cousin Sue during the last couple years of high school and both had boyfriends in the same neighborhood in which Danny lived and worked with Warren.

After high school, Sue and Emma continued to spend time together and it was around this time that Sue, by chance, started to date Warren. Emma however, had already become pregnant from her current boyfriend. She was only nineteen years old and the boyfriend wanted nothing to do with the pregnancy, and promptly left her when he learned of her condition. Suddenly, she found herself in a very difficult situation. She was unemployed and uncertain what the future held for her, let alone what the future would hold for her with a baby. Emma was a young attractive woman, but she felt ashamed of her pregnancy and felt that she had let down her family. She fell into a deep depression and desperately tried to think about how best to handle the situation.

Sue, concerned for her cousin, always tried to get Emma to go out and have some fun, to get her mind off her troubles. One day, she convinced Emma to go out to meet a friend of Warren's in an effort to cheer her up and get her out of the house. Reluctantly, Emma agreed and the two decided to meet Warren and Danny at a garage near the intersection of Lawrence and Western on the north side of Chicago, where the guys were working on a car.

"It was fall, and cool outside," Emma recalls. "Danny immediately struck me as extremely aggressive, and a hustler. I still remember that he was working with Warren on a silver 1966 split-window Corvette; a beautiful car. We were attracted to each other right away, but we both played aloof. Danny had that James Dean, edgy quality to him, which for a young woman at that time was very attractive. Sue asked what I thought [of Danny], but I told her that I didn't want to get into a situation with a guy who was so young and already had two kids."

The fact that Danny was still married and Emma was pregnant didn't stop the instant connection they had together. After talking for awhile, the four of them went into a bar owned by one of Danny's friends. There, they all had a couple drinks and talked.

"It was smoky and dark inside, so we decided to go over to Danny's apartment," Emma recalls. "It was all innocent enough, and that's when I learned the details about his difficult situation with his wife and kids."

Danny told Emma that he really needed someone to look after his children while he worked. The two were very comfortable with each other right from the start, and Emma, who had been looking for a place to stay during her pregnancy agreed to move in to his apartment and watch his kids for him.

"I was ashamed of the pregnancy," Emma remembers of these early days with Danny. "I just wanted to have the baby away from my family. At first, my moving in with Danny was more business than anything else, and it helped us both out at the time. While I was attracted to him, the situation was too difficult to focus on anything romantic between us."

Within a few weeks of this, Warren managed to not only get his own wife pregnant, but he also got Sue pregnant as well. Not surprisingly, Warren refused to leave his wife, forcing Sue to find her own way out of the problem. Emma then became the support mechanism for Sue and at the same time, started to raise and care for Danny's two children, whom she also immediately connected with.

Danny and Emma cared for each other, but due to the difficult circumstances, the romance was limited. Danny and his wife were still trying to sort out what was left of their relationship and Emma realized that she needed more support during her pregnancy.

Three months later, Emma decided to move back in with her family, who had offered her financial assistance as well as much-needed emotional support. She stayed at her parents' house through the remainder of her pregnancy, but still felt lost. She knew she had no way to support the child, and didn't feel that it was right to place the burden of raising a child onto her parents, who had already raised five children of their own. Emma felt that she had no option but to make the heart-wrenching decision to give the child up for adoption. She would admit years later that Danny too, was pushing for that decision, purely to seek control over her. She discussed the situation repeatedly with her family and they agreed to support her in whatever decision that she made.

Not wanting to risk having her baby get sent into an orphanage or have an unknown future, Emma worked with a social worker and found a private adoption agency that worked to find an adoptive couple before the birth.

"I did this so that at least I knew that the baby would go to a loving couple who could support it and give it the best life possible; something that I felt I couldn't give, no matter how much I loved the baby," Emma recalls.

When it came time for the birth, Emma was admitted to the hospital. Since it was a planned adoption, the hospital wouldn't inform her of the sex of the baby and she wasn't even allowed to see it.

"When it came time, I didn't want to sign the paperwork," she remembers. "It is the hardest decision that I have made in my life and felt like I was giving a piece of me away forever. At the last minute, the social worker came in and talked to me. She reminded me of the reasons that I came to this decision and reminded me that this couple was loving, stable, and ready to take the child into their home. They could give the baby what I knew I never could. By me changing my mind, not only would I put this couple back at square one and have to go through the whole process again, but I would also be putting the future of my baby at risk."

Emma reluctantly signed the paperwork and let go of that crucial part of her. She did so in order to ensure that the baby would have the best life possible. But this sacrifice came at a great cost to Emma.

"For the next two days while they kept me in the hospital, I saw all the mothers with their newborns. I could hear the babies crying in the distance, and I lay there, crying too, wondering if one of the babies that I heard was mine; if he or she was ok, cold, or hungry. Did the baby feel the separation that I felt? It was an indescribable pain to feel."

Every year since the birth, Emma has always celebrated the birthday of her baby privately, wondering about whether her child was still living, how he or she was doing, and if she would ever get to see how the baby turned out as an adult. Deep down, she knew she did the right thing given the circumstances of her life at that time. Yet for Emma, it would be years before she was able to move past this experience, and decades before she would finally find answers to her questions about the baby.

CHAPTER 5

Connections

For Danny, the time spent apart from Emma was also difficult. She had moved out and he was trying to balance raising his two children as well as working in order to support them. His wife Barbara was causing him a lot of problems and their fight over custody was getting more and more heated. She began to threaten to take the kids away from Danny and he finally couldn't take it anymore. Under incredible stress, his dark nature took over and one day he approached Barbara and warned her explicitly that if she took his kids from him, "They'll find your body in a fucking dumpster."

It worked. Barbara knew Danny's family history and also knew when he had crossed that invisible line and there was no turning back. With that last straw expressed, Danny was able to keep the children and then rekindled the connection with Emma. Within months, he finalized the divorce with Barbara and moved back in with Emma. Distraught over her decision to give up her baby, Emma enjoyed helping Sue take care of her own baby and welcomed Danny's children as her own, trying desperately to bury the guilt that she felt inside.

Just before Emma had moved back in, Danny had begun to do work with another contact, Ray Pappas, who owned an injection molding company on the north side of Chicago. Ray was another neighborhood contact introduced to Danny by his brothers. Yet unlike Warren, Ray was someone who knew "people."

As Danny's experience grew in Ray's shop, so did his skills. A regular nine-to-five job was simply out of the question for him, and after working together, Ray saw the talent that Danny had and also knew about his family history. Ray felt he was someone to trust who would do well in a more lucrative type of work. In late 1967, Ray introduced Danny to Irwin Weiner, a well-known bail bondsman and alleged Mob financier.

At first, Weiner hired Danny for a couple weeks-worth of carpentry work in the basement of his house. Here, Danny and Irwin got to know each other and Danny discussed his plans for the company he wanted to start. Weiner, when he learned of how lucrative the business could be, quickly offered to secure some investment capital. To Danny, this was exactly what he had been looking for, or at least he thought so at the time. Together, the two men estimated that it would cost around $10,000 to get the business properly up and running, and since Danny didn't have cash on hand but had the industry experience, they made a deal. Irwin would bring in another individual as a "silent" partner, and they would essentially split the ten grand, with Danny owning one third of the company. Each share would equal $3,333 in 1967 (roughly around $24,000[5] in 2013).

At this point, Danny knew perfectly well that Weiner was a connected man. He felt that entering into business with Weiner would not only guarantee some starting capital, but also would guarantee steering some steady business into the company. After all, the Mob doesn't start a business just to have it *not* make money. Even with illegal funds going through the business, on the surface there had to at least appear to be legitimate work going on to cover everything up that was criminal in nature. With Danny's share of the company being based on his knowledge and experience, he felt that there was no way that he could fail. After all, he knew how these things worked from his own family history. His legitimate side of the business would cover anything that his partners would be doing, and he'd make extra cash on top of it. What he didn't realize yet,

---

[5] Dollar Times
http://www.dollartimes.com/calculators/inflation.htm

was exactly the extent that Weiner was connected with powerful, top-level mobsters.

Since it would take time to form the company, Danny kept working on side jobs with Warren and Ray, and became more involved with Emma. For the next several months, Danny built his relationship with Irwin and got to know Weiner's choice for an investor-partner, Mob leader Felix "Milwaukee Phil" Alderisio. Danny began to feel quite empowered, but Warren wasn't happy at all with his friend's new associates. He warned Danny several times to stay away from them; that they were bad news. Danny wouldn't listen, and Warren began to notice a change starting to take place in his friend.

At this time in 1967, "Milwaukee Phil" Alderisio ranked very high in the Chicago Outfit. After learning the details from Danny and Weiner, he wanted to invest in the company for his son, Dominick, and have Dominick help run it. But his son wanted nothing to do with the company; or with his father for that matter. He was appalled at his father's role in the Mob. So much so that he threatened his father with becoming a priest and refused to take any operating role within the company.

Phil still invested, but his son refused to work there. Emma recalls, "I only met Dominick a couple times, and he was never at the factory."

Danny, however, was getting closer to his soon-to-be partners. He and Phil had hit it off right away and the two quickly became close. Emma remembers, "Phil became sort of a father figure to Danny, and it was clear they trusted each other greatly."

Danny was fast becoming the Mob son that Dominick would never be for Phil. In early 1968, the new partners formed International Fiberglass in Elk Grove Village, Illinois, just minutes from Chicago.

Around Emma's 21st birthday in April of 1968, she and Danny discussed details of his new partners' illicit backgrounds.

"I knew who Felix Alderisio was, because he was in the news back then a lot for his Mob involvement," she remembers. "I was nervous about that type of connection, but at the same time, I admit that it was exciting. I was so naïve. There was definitely power in having these guys in business with you and once I got to know them, they seemed like anyone else that we'd been friends with."

With the plans for the new company coming together and the success of that new company on the horizon, Danny asked Emma to marry him. Just prior to the wedding, Weiner invited Danny and Emma to his house for a barbeque. Emma remembers meeting Weiner's wife.

"She was beautiful—an ex-Vegas showgirl—and there we were like in some Mob movie, out back making Pims Cups, a drink that was popular back then, while the guys discussed their business."

For Emma, it felt like she had stepped into another universe. These people had become their friends very quickly and Danny and Emma started getting used to having a lot of money coming in. In August of 1968 they had a simple wedding in a small chapel, and the reception was held in the garage of Emma's parents' house. Each of Danny's partners gave them $100 (around $700[6] in today's value). Weiner was the only partner that showed up for the wedding and Emma remembers that "Irwin wanted a tour of the house as soon as he got there. I thought that was strange since it was such a small house, but looking back, now I'd say that he probably wanted to scope the place out."

After Danny and Emma were married, they were invited several times to Phil's house in Riverside, Illinois, where he would invite Emma to go into another room and select anything she wanted from some "shipments" that had come in. "There were boxes of clothes, and racks of furs. Danny and Phil went and discussed whatever they had to talk about, and there I was with thousands of dollars of women's clothes to choose from," Emma recalls.

"We had a new car constantly, from one of the connected dealerships in the area. I don't remember Danny ever actually paying for a car, or if he did, it was a very low price and he simply paid cash."

---

[6] Dollar Times
http://www.dollartimes.com/calculators/inflation.htm

If there was any remaining doubt how deep Danny was in with the Mob, there would be no doubt left after Danny showed Emma something that signified his connection to them—an unpublished picture and negative of the St. Valentine's Day massacre taken by a Mob-connected photographer just after the shootings. Emma isn't sure if Danny got it from Weiner or Phil, but she clearly understood that her husband was now fully connected. And that image demonstrated their confidence in him. It was clear that Danny was in solid with the top Mobsters in Chicago, and Emma, like it or not, was now along for the ride.

While Emma knew who these men were, Danny still kept a lot of the information about his partners from her. In 1969, "Milwaukee Phil" Alderisio became the leader of the Chicago Outfit. This power only made Danny even cockier than he already was, and the circle of dangerous associates around him began to grow.

Warren, still concerned for his friend, repeatedly warned Danny not to associate with these people, but again Danny refused to listen. He was riding high, had a lot of money, had the clout and power of his connections, and was not about to turn back. Danny's growing list of associates included Angelo "the Hook" LaPietra, top enforcer for the Mob; Joey "Doves" Aiuppa, the Mobster who would eventually take over as Mob leader from Alderisio in 1971[7]; and alleged Mob Capo Joey "the Clown" Lombardo, who came in

---

[7] Organized Crime and Political Corruption
http://www.ipsn.org/a century of chicago mob bosses.htm

to the business around 1969. Danny's son Nick remembers all of his parents' "friends," and recalls that they were accepted like any other family member.

"Uncle Joey [Lombardo} used to take me to the circus and out to lunch all the time. I'd come into the factory to hang out and I'd go with the guys to pick up lunch for everyone."

Danny had found himself in a unique but very dangerous position. Not only had he gone into business with the Mob, but he had also brought them in close to his personal life. They had become family. And through his close connection with Alderisio, he gained an insider's route into Outfit connections rarely seen. There were many dinners with Aiuppa, Alderisio, former Mob Boss Jackie Cerone[8], and other Mob associates at a favorite local Mob restaurant just off River Road near Rosemont Illinois, the Maitre' D. Danny felt untouchable. But these good times would prove to be short-lived. On September 25, 1971, after spending over a year in Federal prison for bank fraud, Alderisio would die, leaving an opening at the top of the Chicago Mob. His death would also leave Danny in an exposed and vulnerable situation.

No longer protected by the top Mob Boss, Danny's respect waned among the other associates. Phil's former influence with

---

[8] Organized Crime and Political Corruption
http://www.ipsn.org/a_century_of_chicago_mob_bosses.htm

International Fiberglass and its other owners was no more, and Lombardo stepped up his role in taking the reins of the company's illegal operations. Danny was quickly losing control of his company and it became clear that his remaining partners were raising the volume of illegal activities to new levels.

"Within months after Phil's death," Emma recalls, "Danny told me how the payroll for International had become astronomical. He knew there was now even more going on than even he knew about, and he became very uneasy about it all."

When the Feds approached Danny at his favorite breakfast place one morning and showed him photographic evidence of his involvement, and then threatened to take him down with his Mob partners if he didn't talk, he knew the good times were over. He could no longer turn to the Mob and he didn't trust the Feds. If what the Feds told him turned out to be true, he was looking at years behind bars for his involvement and at an uncertain future for his family. Additionally, it was looking like Cerone, whom Danny never liked to begin with, was a candidate to take Phil's place as Mob Boss, as he had held the reins prior to Phil's Leadership[9]. This pitted Danny against one of the most powerful men in the Chicago Outfit, and Cerone knew just how much information Danny had on the operations of International Fiberglass, and on all of the gangsters who were involved with it.

---

[9] Ultimately Joseph "Joey Doves" Aiuppa would take over in 1971 and remain in control until 1986, but Cerone took temporary control in the interim while Daniel was at International.

Seemingly overnight Danny found himself completely alone. He needed to figure out how to make his next play to extricate himself, and he refused to be intimidated by either the Mob or the Feds. He wasn't yet convinced that the Feds had enough evidence to convict him, and he knew that he needed to make a definitive statement that rang loud and clear to his partners. Danny decided that the only way to survive this entire situation was to play by the Mob's own rules. It was time that he raised the stakes with his partners and let them know exactly where he stood on the business and with the Feds.

CHAPTER 6

Partners

W hether it was bad luck, fate, or by sheer chance, Danny quickly found himself connected with the top echelon of the Chicago Outfit. While they were definitely not the run-of-the-mill gangsters, these men were also not the flashy, Hollywood Mobsters that most ordinary citizens would envision. True, a couple of them were known for their expensive suits, extravagant ways, or lavish lifestyles, but most would hardly stand out in a crowd. This was intentional so that they wouldn't draw unnecessary attention to themselves. In the Mob, drawing such a level of attention can easily get someone arrested, or worse—killed.

Many of these Mobsters were millionaires many times over, yet most lived in standard, middle-class homes or townhouses in quiet suburbs outside of Chicago. Other than their houses, there were few similarities between the mobsters and their unsuspecting neighbors. These guys had trunk loads of cash hidden in their basements or even inside the walls of their homes. Some would get very creative and add hidden rooms or secret compartments inside the walls to hide guns, money, and other contraband. For instance, Mob executioner "Mad" Sam DeStefano, who lived inconspicuously with his wife and three children in an upper-middle class neighborhood on Chicago's near west side[10], designed a soundproof room in his basement. As the neighbors would sleep blissfully unaware next door, Sam would cheerfully go about his violent work in the privacy of his basement. Many witnesses of Sam's handiwork described his tendency to literally foam at the mouth while torturing his victims, because of how much he enjoyed inflicting pain on people.

"Mad" Sam was close to Danny's associates and especially to Tony "the Ant" Spilotro, who worked directly for Joey "the Clown" Lombardo. Sam's preferred method of torture was to take an ice pick to his victims, who usually were people who couldn't pay the Mob whatever money that they might have owed.

---

[10] Roemer, William F. Jr. *The Enforcer - Spilotro: The Chicago Mob's Man over Las Vegas*. New York: Ivy Books, 1995.

Sam's viciousness was so legendary that even the Mob felt he was completely uncontrollable. No one, even Mobsters, wanted this guy knocking on their door. In 1973, years after Tony Spilotro had worked directly for Sam, learning his ruthless ways, the Mob felt that Sam's uncontrollable nature was about to ruin the chances for Spilotro's beating a murder rap that he was on trial for. The Mob dealt with Sam, someone who couldn't be reasoned with or controlled, the only way they knew how—by killing him. Spilotro in fact, allegedly took Sam out personally by using a shotgun to ensure the job wasn't screwed up. And Spilotro was very good at this type of work; after all, he had learned from the best—"Mad" Sam.[11]

In reality, these seemingly normal-looking men living down the street from the average family were simply killers; cold-blooded, vicious, merciless killers. They could easily have been one's neighbor or the person who owned the pizzeria down the block, but they were also men who wouldn't hesitate to take a blowtorch to someone if they felt that person knew something they needed to know or had something they wanted. And their grip on the city of Chicago is legendary.

A 2005 article in the *Chicago Tribune* reports, "The Chicago Crime Commission counts 1,111 Chicago-area [Mob-related] slayings since 1919, but only 14 have ended in murder convictions and three cases were cleared when the suspected killers were

[11] Roemer, William F. Jr. *The Enforcer - Spilotro: The Chicago Mob's Man over Las Vegas.* New York: Ivy Books, 1995.

murdered before being arrested, according to the commission[12]."
The Mob knows how to operate with impunity in Chicago and to this day, their grip on areas and individuals within the city ensures that few ever get in their way.

In the 1950s and 1960s, the brutality and hard-hitting openness of Mob violence that made Capone famous began to evolve and take on more finesse. The open slayings and brazen violence that had once commonly taken place in the middle of a street, shaking communities all around Chicago, changed to a more muted style as the Mob became more and more sophisticated in its approach to gaining and enforcing its business interests. At the same time, the Feds also became more and more sophisticated in their surveillance of the Mob's activities.

Yet the evolving business model of the Mob also created opportunities for the Mob to blend legitimate business operations with their criminal operations. This resulted in a unique blending of legitimate and illegitimate worlds; a merger that would sometimes draw in unsuspecting entrepreneurs like Danny Seifert.

The Mob would first gain an interest in a legitimate business and then use that business to launder funds, provide fraudulent loans, steer shipments of stolen merchandise, or any other shady

---

[12] "DOJ press release on Major Indictment of Organized Crime Figures." April 25, 2005.
http://www.ipsn.org/indictments/indictments-oc/pr042505-outfit.htm

dealings that would yield a profitable return. Within a short time, the business would become fully Mob-controlled and an ideal front for racketeering, larceny, fraud, intimidation, and in many cases, murder. The Mob even owned interests in healthcare companies that provided coverage services to the Teamsters. These companies like the People's Industrial Consultants in Los Angeles for example, provided kickbacks[13] to key players such as the 1971 Teamsters Boss Frank Fitzsimmons, who happened to be very close to (then) President Richard Nixon and was known to share rides on Air Force One with Nixon.[14] Interestingly, the Teamsters had endorsed Nixon's bid for his 1972 reelection after he pardoned former Teamster Boss Jimmy Hoffa in December 1971.

The moment that Danny signed on with known Mob financier Irwin Weiner, he started down a fatal path with influences far more powerful than he could have ever imagined. And his own self-confidence blinded him to the potential destruction that he would unknowingly face as a Mob pawn.

Initially, Danny's primary partners in the company included Irwin Weiner and Felix Alderisio as principals, but Weiner soon brought in other of his associates to help run it. Mob Capo Joey "the

---

[13] "Bring Your Own." *The Ledger*, May 16, 1973.
http://news.google.com/newspapers?nid=1346&dat=19730516&id=d4
ROAAAAIBAJ&sjid=cvoDAAAAIBAJ&pg=5977,4440055

[14] Gerth, Jeff. "Richard M. Nixon and Organized Crime."
Penthouse, July, 1974.
http://jfk.hood.edu/Collection/Weisberg%20Subject%20Index%20F
iles/N%20Disk/Nixon%20Richard%20M%20President%20Watergate%20F
iles/72-11-
01%20Sundance%20Nixon%20and%20the%20Mafia/Item%2002.pdf

Clown" Lombardo came in as a foreman; bookie Harold Lurie came in to run the finances, and Mob wire-tap and electronics expert Ronald DeAngelis came on board as an "advisor."

DeAngelis was an excellent electronics technician and was known in the underworld for monitoring all police activity on his police scanners. In addition to placing "bugs" for the Mob in key locations, he even successfully "bugged" the Intelligence Bureau of the Chicago Police Department. DeAngelis was also essentially the front line alert system for Mob Boss Sam Giancana. If during his frequent monitoring he heard the police talking about Giancana or even the street that Giancana lived on, a call was placed immediately to the Mob Boss as a warning that he was being monitored or that the police or Feds were on their way.

In 1970, the Feds spotted DeAngelis on a converted Navy minesweeper on Lake Michigan, cruising near the police headquarters. The boat was loaded with surveillance gear, but without being able to prove any wrong doing, the agents could only cite the Mob's electronics whiz for leaking oil into the lake. This citation was later thrown out of court.

DeAngelis, like many others near Seifert, was also in very tight with famed Mob hit-man and enforcer Tony "the Ant" Spilotro. Tony had a reputation as a brutal killer, and his lengthy arrest record included charges for robbery, gambling, and murder. In 1973, a Mob insider gave testimony of the sickening details of a murder committed by Spilotro and a couple of other mobsters: the slaying involved the use of guns and a butcher knife on an individual who was suspected of cheating on the Mob's financial accounts.

But these deadly connections for Danny were just the start. Through these early business partners, Danny was later introduced to more high-profile Mobsters that included John "Jackie the Lackey" Cerone, who would run the Mob from 1966 - 1969[15]; and to hit-man and enforcer Angelo "the Hook" LaPietra, whose nickname came from his method of hanging victims by a meat hook while torturing them.

Of Danny's new associates, Cerone was the one hood who would seem to fit the stereotypical role of a Mobster. He liked to wear expensive suits, intimidated people with his tough attitude and reputation, and no matter who was watching, he did and said whatever he pleased. He also played the part of a gangster to the fullest. A witness described how Cerone would often go into restaurants and ask the waitress what the biggest tip she had that day was, and then throw down a $100 bill, usually followed by some sort of vulgar request that the big tip was supposed to make up for.

The power wielded by Seifert's partners was derived directly from the top of Chicago's organized crime world. Irwin Weiner had made millions through his bail bonds business, where he would also write bonds for the Teamsters Union following the passage of the

---

[15] Organized Crime and Political Corruption
http://www.ipsn.org/a century of chicago mob bosses.htm

Landrum-Griffin Act in 1959[16]. To gain an idea of the scope of his success in the bonds business, one needs to only note that in 1963 Weiner made over an estimated one million dollars from his business with the Teamsters alone. At the time, he had dozens of bond agents working for him, pulling in millions of dollars.

Over the years, Weiner also owned several other Mob-related businesses that included real estate and insurance companies[17]. A short list of Mob businesses that he owned directly or had a major interest would include the Central Casualty Company, United Benefit Fire, Weiner Viola Insurance, Resolute Insurance Company, Titan Management Corp., Summit Fidelity Insurance Company, and Twin Food Products in which he was partnered with none other than Felix Alderisio. This success rate demonstrates how Weiner was considered a high-ranking Mob financier, and someone who knew many key people and could make things happen for those on his good side. However, for those on his bad side, Weiner could also make things happen *to* them rather than *for* them, although he was never convicted for murder.

---

[16] The United States Department of Labor
http://www.dol.gov/compliance/laws/comp-lmrda.htm
[17] "Executive Session Testimony before the House Select Committee on Assassinations - Irwin Weiner."
http://jfkassassination.net/russ/m_j_russ/weiner.htm

Weiner grew up with Paul "Red" Dorfman (a former Al Capone associate), who was the father of Allen Dorfman. Allen was installed as the head advisor of the Teamsters Central States Pension Fund's Health and Welfare claims by the legendary Jimmy Hoffa, in return for Allen's father helping Hoffa to win support from the Chicago Outfit during his rise as the Teamsters Boss. The Mob basically ensured Hoffa's role in running the Teamsters.

Through Paul Dorfman, Weiner met Jimmy Hoffa, a meeting that would not only build a business relationship, but also a very lucrative partnership with the Teamsters in which Weiner was guaranteed the position to provide bonds to both Hoffa and the Teamsters Union. Back then, Weiner, Dorfman, and Spilotro were known for flying around the country in Dorfman's $2.9 million private jet, bought in part with funds secured from none other than Frank Sinatra, and the rest paid for through a convenient loan obtained from the Teamsters Pension Funds.

In addition to these connections, Weiner also had dealings with Earl Ruby, the older brother of famed assassin Jack Ruby, who killed Lee Harvey Oswald. Ruby worked as a Teamsters Union organizer for about a year under Weiner's friend and associate, Paul Dorfman. Earl and Irwin had gone to school together as kids, and this lifelong connection would eventually land Weiner in front of the JFK Subcommittee hearing on May 18, 1978, to testify in the ongoing investigation into the assassination of President John F. Kennedy[18].

This testimony by Weiner helped to fuel conspiracy theorists' ideas regarding the Mob's involvement in Kennedy's murder for decades—and rightly so. Throughout his testimony, Weiner casually and flippantly answered questions that not only showed Jack Ruby called Weiner just before the assassination, but also that Weiner had been in meetings in Cuba years prior with top Mob leaders. "I guess they were all pleasure," was Weiner's off-handed response when he was pressed by the Feds as to the nature of his trips to Cuba with various Mobsters. During this time period, the Mob was less than pleased with Kennedy's crackdown on organized crime and especially with his insertion of Title 1 of the Landrum-Griffin Act when he was a senator, which gave the government tools to better fight union corruption and was intended to give greater transparency to the union's financial records. This was deemed a major blow to the Mob, which used the Union's Pension funds as a personal ATM with which to provide fraudulent loans to Mob interests and Mob leaders.

The true scale of Weiner's self-confidence and power was more than apparent during his testimony, as he chose to represent

---

[18] "Executive Session Testimony before the House Select Committee on Assassinations - Irwin Weiner." http://jfkassassination.net/russ/m_j_russ/weiner.htm

himself without even having a lawyer present. Representing oneself without an attorney while being questioned about one's possible role into the murder of the President of the United States takes one hell of a lot of confidence, and he did so successfully. The following excerpt is taken directly from Weiner's statement during the executive session of the JFK Subcommittee Hearing, May 18, 1978, and demonstrates his control over the questioning about his possible relationship with Jack Ruby, and also his interaction and overall confidence with Federal Investigators:

[EXECUTIVE SESSION]
JFK SUBCOMMITTEE HEARING
TUESDAY, MAY 18, 1978
HOUSE OF REPRESENTATIVES,
SELECT COMMITTEE ON ASSASSINATIONS,
JOHN F. KENNEDY SUBCOMMITTEE,
Washington, D.C.

The subcommittee met at 9 :25 a.m., pursuant to notice, in room 1310, Longworth House Office Building, Hon. Richardson J. Preyer (chairman of the subcommittee) presiding.
Present: Representatives Preyer (presiding), Dodd, Fithian, and Sawyer.
Also present: G. Cornwell, J. Hornbeck, J. McDonald, A. Purdy, J. Wolf, II. Shapiro, E. Berning, T. Hutton, M. Ewing, A. Taylor, R. Morrison, L. Svendsen, D. Billings, and W.H. Cross.

Mr. WOLF - Mr. Weiner, the first area of questions will concern your relationship with Jack Ruby. For the committee members this is listed on tab 2 of the briefing book. When was the first time you met Jack Ruby, Mr. Weiner.?
Mr. WEINER - I don't know. I don't remember. I went to school with his brother, Earl. Jack was a little older than I was. I might

have met Jack Ruby four or five times in my life.

Mr. WOLF - What is the first time you recall?

Mr. WEINER - I can't recall.

Mr. WOLF - Did you know him in high school?

Mr. WEINER - I don't remember.

Mr. WOLF - Did you meet him prior to 1960 which was the election of President Kennedy?

Mr. WEINER - Oh, yes.

Mr. WOLF - Did you meet him prior to 1950?

Mr. WEINER - It could have been.

Mr. WOLF - Do you recall--

Mr. WEINER - I would say I met him probably in the 1930's.

Mr. WOLF - What were the circumstances of your first meeting?

Mr. WEINER - It was an older brother of a friend of mine, not even a good friend. Somebody I knew.

Mr. WOLF - You are speaking of Earl?

Mr. WEINER - Yes.

Mr. WOLF - You met Earl in high school?

Mr. WEINER - Right.

Mr. WOLF - Were you friendly with Earl?

Mr. WEINER - Yes.

Mr. WOLF - Did you meet other members of the Ruby family?

Mr. WEINER - I don't think I did.

Mr. WOLF - Were you ever to the Ruby house?

Mr. WEINER - I don't believe I was.

Mr. WOLF - How much older than yourself was Jack Ruby?

Mr. WEINER - I don't have any idea. I know he was a few years older.

Mr. WOLF - You testified that you believe you met him four or five times in total, is that correct?

Mr. WEINER - Probably.

Mr. WOLF - What meetings with Jack Ruby do you remember?

Mr. WEINER - I don't remember any of them.

Mr. WOLF - How do you know you met him four or five times?

Mr. WEINER - I am assuming I met him four or five times. I saw him with his brother, spoke to him a few times. I am only going back-- you are talking about 30-some years or 40 years.

Mr. WOLF - All your contacts with Jack Ruby were during the 1930's?

Mr. WEINER - No.

Mr. WOLF - When were your other contacts with Jack Ruby?

Mr. WEINER - He called me up one time.

Mr. WOLF - When was that?

Mr. WEINER - I don't remember. It was in the sixties, prior to the assassination of the President.

Mr. WOLF - How much prior to the assassination?

Mr. WEINER - I don't have any idea.

Mr. WOLF - You do recollect that call?

Mr. WEINER - Yes. I recollect that call because I have had a lot of problems because of that call.

Mr. WOLF - Was that call on October 26, 1963?

Mr. WEINER - It could have been.

Mr. WOLF - One month prior to the assassination?

Mr. WEINER - It could have been.

Mr. WOLF - At what time previous to that call do you recollect seeing Jack Ruby?

Mr. WEINER - Maybe 10 or 15 years prior to that.

Mr. WOLF - Ten or fifteen years prior to the call?

Mr. WEINER - Correct.

Mr. WOLF - Why do you characterize yourself as having a lot of trouble concerning that call?

Mr. WEINER - I tell you what problem I have and the reason for my attitude. Evidently as a result of this call an agent called my house.

Mr. WOLF - FBI agent?

Mr. WEINER - Yes. An FBI agent called my house and spoke to my daughter. It was right after Oswald was killed. He spoke to my daughter and asked where I was. I was in Florida at the time. She didn't know where I was. She had just come in from school. She told the agent she didn't know where I was but expected to hear from me. Called the next day. She was shaking with fright because the agent had told her he wanted to talk to me about the assassination of the President. As a result of that, anytime anybody came and talked to me I dismissed them.

Mr. WOLF - The FBI did contact you regarding that call?

Mr. WEINER - Yes. I never spoke to them about it.

Mr. WOLF - The reason you are not speaking--

Mr. WEINER - Is because of the way they mistreated my daughter.

Mr. WOLF - Did they mistreat your daughter?

Mr. WEINER - That is the extent of it. They scared her to death.

Mr. WOLF - You felt you should not speak to the FBI about the assassination of President Kennedy?

Mr. WEINER - You are 100 percent right.

Mr. WOLF - Did anybody else ever contact you regarding that call?

Mr. WEINER - Newspaper people. I refused to speak to them. A couple of your investigators.

Mr. WOLF - You refused to speak to our investigators; is that correct?

Mr. WEINER - Right.

Mr. WOLF - What was discussed during that phone call?

Mr. WEINER - Jack Ruby called me. Evidently he had a nightclub in Dallas, Tex. He had a striptease night, one night a week he had an amateur striptease. Some union that was affiliated with entertainers had stopped him. They asked him to stop because the amateur entertainers were not members of the union. He stopped and another competitor of his opened up. He called me and wanted to know if I would write a bond. He was looking to get an injunction. The lawyer told him if he got an injunction he would have to put up a bond. He asked me if I would do that and I told him no. Then he told me he was going to file a lawsuit. That was the extent of our conversation. It was just in relation to that. I never heard from him since and I have never heard from him prior to that.

Mr. WOLF - You had no contact with him prior to that time?

Mr. WEINER - Absolutely no.

Mr. WOLF - How did Jack Ruby come to call you?

Mr. WEINER - Through his brother. That was my business,

writing bonds. I don't have any idea.

Mr. WOLF - Why did you refuse to write the bond that. He requested?

Mr. WEINER - I didn't have the authority to write it.

Mr. WOLF - Did you direct him to somebody who did?

Mr. WEINER - No.

Mr. WOLF - Your testimony was that was the business you were in at that time?

Mr. WEINER - I still am.

Mr. WOLF - Why do you say you had no authority to write a bond?

Mr. WEINER - If I remember correctly I don't think the company was authorized to do business in Texas. I just didn't want to get involved in it. There was no way I could do it.

Mr. WOLF - Did you ever refer him to somebody in Texas? Could you have referred him to somebody in Texas?

Mr. WEINER - I don't know anybody in Texas who would write a bond.

Mr. WOLF - You don't do business with any firm in Texas?

Mr. WEINER - Not that I know of.

Mr. WOLF - What else was discussed during that conversation?

Mr. WEINER - That is all that was discussed.

Mr. WOLF - And that conversation, do you recollect how long it lasted?

Mr. WEINER - I don't have any idea.

Mr. WOLF - You had no contacts for 15 years previous to that call with Jack Ruby?

Mr. WEINER - I never had contact with Jack Ruby, never socially. Never went with him anywhere, never broke bread with him, never had anything to do with Jack Ruby at any time in my life.

Mr. WOLF - What was the contact 15 years prior to that phone call with Jack Ruby?

Mr. WEINER - How the hell do I know?

Mr. WOLF - You testified

Mr. WEINER - I am just guessing. It could have been 30 years before. I don't remember.

Mr. WOLF - What other contact with Jack Ruby do you remember?

Mr. WEINER I didn't have any contacts with him.
Mr. WOLF - Did you ever meet with him?
Mr. WEINER - I told you I never met with him, never had coffee with him, never went to his house, never had lengthy conversation with him that I remember.
Mr. WOLF - Except that one phone call?
Mr. WEINER - Except that one phone call.

During the testimony, Weiner's confirmed links to Jimmy Hoffa, the Teamsters Union, and Allen Dorfman were also raised:

Mr. WOLF - Have you ever met with Jimmy Hoffa?
Mr. WEINER - Yes.
Mr. WOLF - What were the circumstances of your first meeting?
Mr. WEINER - Writing a bond for the Teamsters International under the Landrum-Griffin Act.
Mr. WOLF - When was that?
Mr. WEINER - It would be around 1959.
Mr. WOLF - Who else was present at that meeting?
Mr. WEINER - Probably Allen Doffman [sic].
Mr. WOLF - Who introduced you to Mr. Hoffa?
Mr. WEINER - Allen Dorfman.
Mr. WOLF - What was discussed at that meeting?
Mr. WEINER - Getting a bond placed. He was having a problem.
Mr. WOLF - Was it one bond?
Mr. WEINER - It was a bond that covered the international. It covered each officer of each local that represented, that was a

member of the Teamsters International.[19]

While always suspected of his involvement, the government had no proof of Weiner's role and nothing to tie him to the assassination. After this executive session, Weiner was never questioned again.

But evidence and suspicion of Irwin Weiner's JFK involvement would continue into modern day when Danny's grown son Nick Seifert would, in 2001 and 2002, receive denials of his requests for information by the US Department of Justice in relation to files and records on his father's murder.

The records have been transferred to the National Archives and Records Administration (NARA) pursuant to the President John F. Kennedy Assassination Records Collection Act of 1992 (The JFK Act). Therefore, these files are no longer in our possession. Transmission of these records is mandated by the JFK Act and public access to them is available through NARA.

The Feds knew that Weiner's friends and business associates were part of an intricate network of Mobsters. They knew that his dealings with them went far beyond their businesses in Chicago, and stretched all the way to Las Vegas and Cuba where he shared in illegal gambling operations. In the late 1950s Weiner would make several trips to Cuba with friends Allen Dorfman and Seifert's other partner,

---

[19] "Executive Session Testimony before the House Select Committee on Assassinations - Irwin Weiner."
http://jfkassassination.net/russ/m_j_russ/weiner.htm

Felix Alderisio. There, they would meet with Florida Mob Boss Sam Trafficante and none other than Chicago Mob Boss Sam Giancana. Not surprisingly, Jack Ruby was also in Cuba several times in 1959, the same year Weiner and his Mob friends were there having meetings. Weiner refused to admit that Ruby had any meetings with him or his Mob associates and claimed to have no knowledge of Ruby's activities while he was there.

Weiner also grew up in Chicago as a childhood friend of Felix "Milwaukee Phil" Alderisio. Rumored to have gotten his nickname after "filling" a target's guts with seventeen bullets during a hit for Giancana in Milwaukee Wisconsin, Alderisio was one of the top members of the Chicago Mob and a man whom everyone feared—a known, ruthless hit man. With Alderisio coming on board at International Fiberglass, life would change forever for Danny.

Alderisio's involvement with the Mob went back to the days of Capone, where as a teenager he would hang around Capone's headquarters and try to get work as a messenger for the famed criminal. During his teens, he was rumored to have been a member of the 42 Gang; the same gang in which future Mob leaders Sam Giancana and Sam "Teetz" Battaglia, as well as notorious Mob-executioner "Mad" Sam DeStefano were all members. Based out of a tough Sicilian neighborhood on Chicago's west side, the 42s were a local Chicago street gang that did the low-end work for Capone's organization back in the early 1900s. Operating as enforcers for the smaller loans or for street-level intimidation work, the gang was known to be the proving grounds for many up-and-coming Chicago Mobsters.

Alderisio eventually found steady work in the Mob via his cousin, Louis "Cock-eyed" Fratto, a known labor racketeer and Outfit member. Once he joined them, Phil quickly rose through the Mob ranks becoming an enforcer for bosses such as Sam "Teetz" Battaglia. As his status increased, he became involved with delivering payoffs to Chicago judges, lawyers, and police who were on the Mob's payroll.

By the 1950s, Alderisio was a definite "heavy" in the organization and was someone that people rightly feared. In 1962, he was one of four Mobsters (including "Mad" Sam and Tony Spilotro) involved in an infamous torture incident, where they placed the head of their victim in a vice and tightened it to the point where his eyes popped out of their sockets. Alderisio and his associates did this so that they could find out the location of another "rat," which they felt had crossed the Mob by performing an unauthorized murder. This incident was made famous in the Hollywood movie *Casino*[20], in a scene where Joe Pesci's character who was based on Tony Spilotro, inflicted the vice torture on a victim.

On July 24, 1975, the Wall Street Journal reported the events of the murder of Danny Seifert and the subsequent failure to convict

---

[20] IMDB http://www.imdb.com/title/tt0112641/

several individuals whom the Government had been observing for years. Of these, although already dead, Alderisio and his Mob reputation were highlighted first:

Felix "Milwaukee Phil" Alderisio, the most active Mafia boss in Chicago, who had once been overheard by FBI bugs as he boasted of murder and who was known to police as "the king of scam," scam being the planned bankruptcy of supposedly legitimate businesses.[21]

Alderisio's long association with the Mob linked him to top Mob bosses Sam Giancana and Tony Accardo. Accardo, also known as "Joe Batters," was viewed for decades as the "Chairman of the Board" of the Chicago Outfit, and was looked upon as royalty in the world of the Mafia. His early ties also went straight to Al Capone, back when he worked as a bodyguard and enforcer for the infamous Chicago gangster. Accardo had gotten the nickname, "Joe Batters" after he had beaten a couple of Capone's adversaries to death with a baseball bat when a murder plot against Capone had been discovered. Accardo's rise to the top was legendary, and by 1944 he stepped into the role of acting boss under Consigliore Paul "the Waiter" Ricca after Ricca had been sent away to prison. Accardo would remain in this command role all the way until 1957 when his

---

[21] The Wall Street Journal Archives
http://pqasb.pqarchiver.com/wsj/advancedsearch.html

own protégé' Sam Giancana would step in to take over, once Accardo had "retired." But even though Accardo had retired from the daily activities of a Boss, the reporting structure stayed the same; Giancana technically still reported to Accardo, and Ricca still advised on all Mob affairs.

Giancana was another Capone-era hood and had served as a driver and shooter for the infamous gangster. As a teenager, he had also been the leader of the notorious 42 gang. However, Giancana's real brilliance was in numbers and gambling. He had first approached Accardo in the 1940s with a plan to take over the numbers rackets in the black neighborhoods on the south side of Chicago. By using the brutally effective tactics of intimidation and murder, Giancana succeeded in his quest, and the payoff for his efforts was his gaining full control of the street rackets, which was a very lucrative business for the Mob. But this was just the start of a steady, incremental increase in gambling interests that would take Giancana from controlling local underground gambling joints in Chicago neighborhoods like Cicero and Calumet City, to full-blown casinos in Cuba (before Castro's takeover), and ultimately, Las Vegas.

Yet Giancana would not have the long reign as a Mob leader that Accardo enjoyed, in part due to the advances in surveillance technology used by the Feds. By 1963 he was being monitored 24/7 by the FBI, and in 1965 he was sentenced to one year in prison for refusing to testify in front of a grand jury regarding organized crime activities in Chicago. By this time however, his leadership had already been questioned by those within the Mob, and in 1966 he was officially deposed by the Mob as its leader. Just after this humiliation, Giancana fled to Mexico in self-imposed exile, officially marking the end of any long-term, top-boss rule within the Mob leadership.

Giancana was replaced briefly by Sam "Teetz" Battaglia, who was tried and then imprisoned for racketeering shortly after taking control. John "Jackie the Lackey" Cerone next would take over for a couple of years, but then the leadership was claimed by none other than Felix Alderisio in 1969, not long after Seifert partnered with him and Irwin Weiner. This unprecedented level of elite-mobster connections made the situation all the more exciting and compelling for Danny. After all, who wouldn't feel empowered when his business partners could exert global influence and were leaders of the most powerful organized crime syndicate in the country?

However, Alderisio too, would only be in charge a short time before he also ended up going to prison in 1970 on charges of attempting to defraud a suburban Chicago bank. He died in 1971 while incarcerated in the Marion, Illinois Penitentiary. At Alderisio's funeral, the Feds observed all levels of Mobsters attending, as high up to and including Accardo; a mass gangster turn-out to pay their respects. Emma and Danny also attended, and while she doesn't recall seeing Accardo, she does remember that it was "filled with lots of men who really fit the profile of a Mobster." Danny even joked to Emma, "When we pulled up to the service the FBI probably took down our license plate."

Alderisio's death not only left an opening in the Outfit, but also created uncertainty for Seifert, since his main connection, mentor, and source of protection was now history. Unluckily for Danny, it was another of his remaining business partners, Joey "the Clown" Lombardo, who would become the linchpin that decided Danny's fate after the death of Alderisio.

"The Clown" earned his nickname early in his criminal career, traceable to his habit of constantly joking around and his inclinations to make funny faces during police mug shots after he had been arrested. Friends of Lombardo's have stated (and even Emma remembers) that Lombardo was always the one to be able to make a tense situation light by his antics. When arrested, he did funny mug shots purposely so as to be more unrecognizable by the cops, later when he was out on the streets. This was hardly an effective ploy and only set him apart from the other mobsters, as he had become a well-recognized figure in the Chicago Mob, by gangsters and police alike.

Joey Lombardo has never admitted to being a Mob boss or even to being associated with the Mob, for that matter. He was born around the prime of Capone's rule in 1929. Just another street kid like his future partners, Lombardo grew up running scams, playing cards, pitching pennies (the only "crime" he's ever admitted to), and other very juvenile ways of getting in trouble with the law. Yet as he grew older, these petty crimes evolved to theft, gambling, and intimidation.

By the 1950s, Lombardo had allegedly joined the Chicago Mob and had begun running the "juice" loans (or street tax) from local businesses. Juice loans amount to basically shaking down local business owners for protection money on a monthly or weekly basis. The Mob would "squeeze" a target to get the "juice" out of them, and Lombardo's toughness made him especially effective. If the business owners felt that they didn't need protection, the Mob simply created the need for that protection by having someone they hired come in and either rob the place, beat the owner up, or threaten his family, etc. It didn't take much to have them cave in and start the payouts to a Mob collector.

By 1963, Lombardo had been arrested multiple times, the latest of which was for kidnapping and loan sharking. But "the Clown" would prove hard to convict; all of his arrests and trials to this point ended in acquittals, due to the Mob's control over Cook County judges. By the late 1960s, Lombardo was a known Mob heavy and was tied to Mobsters like Jackie Cerone, Tony Spilotro, Felix Alderisio, his own cousin, Joe "the Builder" Andriacchi (another high-ranking Mob associate), among many others. Lombardo had spent years honing his specialties, which included intimidation, loan sharking, and fraud. In particular, he was given the important job of handling the fraudulent loans from the Teamsters Union and the Laborers Union to fund gambling interests in Las Vegas, a setup from which the Mob would successfully siphon millions of dollars a year from mobbed-up casinos such as the Stardust, the Riviera, and several others. They also created fake businesses that would be given multiple "loans" from the Teamsters, only to have the money land in the pockets of Chicago Mob bosses.

Up until Alderisio's death, the Seiferts were close to Lombardo. However, once Danny had left International, he would learn first-hand about Lombardo's skills. Under Orders from the top, "The Clown" began his intimidation efforts against Seifert to keep him from talking.

One incident in 1972 involved Lombardo sitting in a car in front of the Seiferts' house at the time of day when Danny's children were supposed to be coming home from school. Emma saw Lombardo, immediately called the police and then grabbed her gun and rushed her children upstairs into a closet to hide. The police contacted Danny, who drove to the Bensenville Police Station to fill out an incident report, in which the lead investigator noted for the record that "Lombardo has the reputation of being a 'hit' man for the mob." Danny arrived home later that evening with a full police escort, surrounded by multiple officers and FBI agents in plain clothes, several of whom were carrying shotguns hidden in their trench coats.

For Lombardo, being a "hit man" was far more than just a reputation. He was implicated in having direct involvement with at least six murders during his career, and most crime experts agree there were many more murders not accounted for.

At a later trial in 1985, Ken Eto, a former Mob insider who ran the Chinatown gambling rings, would come forward and describe Lombardo and Alderisio in detail. Eto had the unfortunate luck to be shot in the head three times by the Mob only to survive and flip, and become a top informant against them. In the trial, he described Alderisio as "violent and very dangerous." When asked about his potential for murder, Eto replied simply, "He would kill in an instant."[22] Lombardo was described by Eto as ranking just below Joey Aiuppa and Jackie Cerone, and Eto made reference to the fact that Lombardo was "made." And there is only one way to be considered made in the Mob. You had to kill for them.

In 1974, Lombardo would be charged with embezzlement of $1.4 million from the Pension funds of the Teamsters Union, along with Allen Dorfman, Tony Spilotro, Irwin Weiner, and Ron DeAngelis. The key witnesses in the investigation were to be Danny Seifert and Harold Lurie, both of whom were being pressured by the

---

[22] Roemer, William F. *The Enforcer - Spilotro: The Chicago Mob's Man over Las Vegas*. New York: Ivy Books, 1995. p. 249-250

Feds to discuss the Mob operations within International Fiberglass. When Seifert was killed just before the trial was to begin, Lurie came down with a sudden case of amnesia on the stand and all five Mobsters ended up walking. What the defendants hadn't realized was that Lurie had worked with the IRS for two years, documenting their transactions and conspiracy. Yet, even with Lurie's insider proof, his silence while on the stand allowed all of the men to walk free.

Years later in 1982, Lombardo would once again be charged, this time with extortion and bribery along with Allen Dorfman in what was a Federal investigation called, Operation PENDORF (Penetration of Dorfman).[23] But this time, the Mob was concerned that Dorfman was too weak-hearted to stand up to prison, and felt that he was ready to talk to the Feds. On January 20, 1983, Dorfman and Irwin Weiner met outside of a hotel near Chicago, preparing to go to lunch when a gunman came up and shot Dorfman in the head several times. Weiner walked away unharmed. Not surprisingly, Weiner was suspected of setting up Dorfman to ensure he didn't talk and Lombardo was suspected of being directly involved with the murder. Tony the "Ant" Spilotro was suspected as being the triggerman. None of this, of course, was ever proven. Because Dorfman was gunned down, the head of the Chicago Crime

23 Russo, Gus. The Outfit: The Role of Chicago's Underworld in the Shaping of Modern America. New York: Bloomsbury, 2004. p.487

Commission stated in 1983, "A lot of people in the criminal world will sleep better tonight knowing that Dorfman is silenced."[24] And that parallel to Seifert's murder as the Mob's answer to the risk of standing trial, cannot be understated.

Lombardo would eventually be convicted in 1985 of skimming millions of dollars from Las Vegas casinos between 1974 and 1978. He was sentenced to 15 years, and was later paroled in 1992. Upon leaving prison, he noticed articles in the newspapers speculating on his role in the Chicago Mob, with many people suspecting that Lombardo was being primed to become the next big boss. This prompted him to take out an article of his own in the newspaper stating:

> I am Joe Lombardo, I have been released on parole from federal prison.
> I never took a secret oath with guns and daggers, pricked my finger, drew blood, or burned paper to join a criminal organization. If anyone hears my name used in conjunction with any criminal activity, please notify the FBI and my parole officer, Ron Kumke.[25]

---

[24] Malcolm, Andrew H. "Dorfman, Teamster Advisor Slain; Faced Long Term Bribery Case." *New York Times*, January 21, 1983. http://www.nytimes.com/1983/01/21/us/dorfman-teamster-adviser-slain-faced-long-term-bribery-case.html

[25] Russo, Gus. *The Outfit: The Role of Chicago's Underworld in the Shaping of Modern America*. New York: Bloomsbury, 2004. p.475

Ultimately, the Seiferts would see some level of justice for Danny's death when, on April 27, 2005, fourteen people were indicted including Lombardo and Frank "the German" Schweihs for the murders of Danny Seifert and seventeen other victims.[26] Lombardo fled and was on the run for almost eight months, until he was finally captured by FBI agents in Elmwood Park, Illinois on January 13, 2006.

The scope of the trial revealed clearly that the individuals Danny had found himself involved with were far more than just business partners, and more than just run-of-the-mill mobsters. At first, they had been considered good friends by Danny and Emma, which only made them even more dangerous because of how their closeness inspired trust. But this friendship would prove manipulative and short-lived, and once Danny realized that he could not control his partners or their take-over activities, he became a dangerous liability to the Mob as well as a potentially great asset to the FBI. He knew and had seen far too much for the Mob's comfort and their patience was running out. For Danny, the beginning of the downward spiral was Alderisio's death, when he suddenly found himself unprotected and vulnerable to the new leadership. Danny knew he was in trouble, but neither he nor Emma truly understood the level of danger that they were about to confront.

---

26 Operation Family Secrets Press Release
http://www.justice.gov/usao/iln/pr/chicago/2005/pr0425_01.pdf

CHAPTER 7

The Fall

The success that Danny quickly gained when he first started working with Alderisio and Weiner was far from a harbinger of his devastating future. Danny had recently married, he was away from his first wife, he had his two children living with him, and he had money--a lot of money. Things looked very good for the young, mobbed-up entrepreneur. Yet what showed on the surface in his life was far different from the change that was taking place within Danny. It was as if his very being was irresistibly drawn to the dark forces that were beginning to influence him and his future.

Danny's oldest son Nick remembers that when he was a young boy, "Dad was always joking around. He was a very strict father, but he also had a lot of fun with us too."

However, that fun-loving persona would begin to change. Emma could never have imagined the dynamic shift that would take place within him in just a few years. Looking back, she acknowledges that she was nervous when she first found out just who Danny's partners were. But once Emma got to really know all the people involved personally with Danny, she began to feel more and more comfortable because they were always generous and affable.

"You never knew about any of the scary stuff with these guys," she recalls. "There were certainly rumors and stories you'd see on TV, but they were just our friends at that point and the kids liked them too. The violent stories you read now, seemed impossible to me at that time; so as difficult as it sounds, it was hard to imagine the potential for violence with these guys."

But this "impossibility" of violence from these likeable guys was not the case. At that time, Felix Alderisio was known by the authorities to have been directly involved with multiple murders. Ironically, for Danny, this couldn't have been more of a blessing, at least in his mind. The void left by Alderisio's own son created an "adoptive" opening for Danny, and right away the two became very close, which led to immediate power rubbing off on Danny's in the form of mobster's clout. He ate it up. His toughness and cockiness were the perfect clay for Alderisio to mold, and Danny was more than willing to learn the ways of the Mob that had been lost to him after his own father had died.

Danny decided to keep the business' dealings to himself and to only tell Emma very limited pieces of information. Quite simply, Danny had nothing else that he was good at. Without these partners, there was no way for him to get the capital that he needed to start a large business that would make the money he felt was necessary for his family, not to mention the plush lifestyle that he sought. He wanted the good life that he perceived his father had once enjoyed, but he also wanted far more: the power of knowing influential and important people, even if those people were gangsters.

However, once Danny was in with Alderisio, he quickly learned that there were bigger plans in the works for his fiberglass business. The men with whom he had become involved had a viscously sure-fire recipe for success that had nothing to do with operating a small-time legitimate business. That front was simply a cover for their real interests, which would net millions to those who ruled at the top. Danny was told of new plans to take out impressive "legitimate" business loans through their contact at The Teamsters Union, Allen Dorfman. These loans would be immediately approved, no questions asked, and would not be tracked by the union in any real sense, thanks to Dorfman's influential control. This allowed for the business' owners to skim money off the original loan amount, default on the loans and not have to repay them, as well as split any actual profits that came in through real business, which Danny was in charge of, and for which he got his cut.

For taking part in the fraud, Danny would be provided a bonus perk: a monthly payment besides what he'd normally make in his own legitimate pursuance of business. This side of the business operations was never revealed to Emma, who simply thought the investments from Weiner and Alderisio had grown the company and secured the much-increased level of business for Danny to start making real money. His agreement with his partners allowed him to take part in that lucrative skim.

Danny's brother Bob was also involved with International Fiberglass at first, and knew DeAngelis previously through his own connections. DeAngelis, Dorfman, Lombardo, Weiner, Spilotro, and two others were all eventually indicted on February 18, 1974, for defrauding the Teamsters Central States Pension Funds.

But the loans going through International Fiberglass from the Teamsters were also really the illicit coffers of two companies in New Mexico, the American Pail Company and Gaylur Products Inc. Another Mob front, American Pail was the company that Bob was supposed to help run, along with DeAngelis and Lombardo, who were also responsible for Gaylur Products. The continually insolvent American Pail Company and Gaylur Products would end up being the linchpins of the Fed's investigation into the fraudulent loans secured from the Central States Fund, and would end up being the paper-trail catalyst that led investigators to International Fiberglass, ultimately resulting in the murder of Danny Seifert.

Once the Feds dug into the unsecured loan practices with American Pail, they realized it was the tip of the iceberg. Those who were authorizing the loans to American Pail had also authorized loans to other insolvent companies in Deming, going all the way back to 1959. All told, the mobsters funneled approximately $6 million over 15 years. Yet the Feds only focused on the $1.4 million siphoned since 1971 through American Pail, Gaylur Products, and International Fiberglass for the 1974 indictments.[27]

As the loans started flowing freely into American Pail from the Teamsters, the company's front was established and Bob's role was no longer needed. This shift led him to begin working with Danny part time in the fiberglass company, with the same lucrative scam intentions as the fake pail company had been for Bob.

Danny's murder eventually prevented any evidence from the loan pipeline at International coming to light for the trial, but the links between his partners, the Teamsters' fraud, American Pail, and the murder can't be ignored. Once Danny had gotten in with

---

[27] "Joseph Lombardo." La Cosa Nostra Database.
http://www.lacndb.com/php/Info.php?name=Joseph%20Lombardo

Alderisio and Weiner and the business model for success was spelled out to him, he quickly agreed to be involved.

It is arguable if Danny really had a choice at that point, but the basic reality is that it was far too much money for him to ignore or refuse. Danny was pulling in a hefty amount for simply "looking the other way." This led to a lot of extra spending money for the Seiferts. Cars were obtained from Mob-related car dealers who would let Danny pick any car from the lot for free, or close to it. These cars were then removed from the showroom listing and simply deleted from the dealer's inventory. There were other soft perks as well, such as being able to show up at any connected high-priced restaurant at any time without a reservation and not having to wait. Nick was old enough to remember some of the perks that trickled down to him as one of Danny's children.

"I remember Uncle Joey [Lombardo] took me and my sis to the circus one day. It was cold and rainy outside, and there was a huge line. Joey just walked up to the guy letting people in, and he opened the gate for us and we walked right in and had the best seats in the house, right up front. I had no idea who Joey was other than "Uncle Joey," but to a little kid, I thought it was really cool that he was able to get us in like that, and not have to wait in the rain."

But it was another of Nick's memories that would hint at the real side of "uncle" Joey Lombardo.

"Down the street from Dad's factory was a place called the Beef and Barrel, where the guys used to get their lunches from all the time. I'd go in and help dad around the factory and would sometimes go on the lunch runs with the guys. Lombardo took me with him one day, and when we got there, he started arguing with the owner. I don't remember the details, but I do remember that it had to do with him owing Lombardo money. Looking back, it was probably protection tax or a "juice" loan, but I was just a kid at the time, and didn't know what was going on. It got really heated and I remember Joey told him, 'Fuck you,' and he grabbed the food and left. Not long after that argument, the Beef and Barrel burned down. I remember that, because dad actually made the plastic food trays for them. They were shaped like a steer's horns on the sides. The restaurant was rebuilt and a while later, Lombardo and I again went in to grab lunch for the factory. Same thing: a big argument ending with Lombardo yelling, 'Fuck you' and leaving, and then shortly thereafter, the place burned down again; but this time it was never rebuilt."

Nick later retold this story to the FBI, who allegedly corroborated the facts with historical fire records from the town. The fact that Nick was young, but still old enough to hang out at the factory, sometimes allowed him to see things behind the scenes that even Emma had no idea were occurring. Because of this, Nick is the one that can speak of things that were often hidden from the rest of the family.

"Dad used to tell me straight to my face, 'Don't fucking talk about what you know,' and that was clear enough for me," Nick Remembers. "It helped, of course, that I really didn't know what was going on. I was young enough not to understand, but also old enough to notice that things were not normal. They would register to me, but it would be much later in life that I would start to put two-and-two together."

Things had begun to take a new direction for Danny, but this new direction also began to change him. The Danny that joked around and played pranks on people began to slowly fade.

"He began to become more and more strict with us, and began to get very rough with me in particular," Nick recalls.

Emma also noticed this change in her husband. "Danny's temper would flare, especially when Nick would get in trouble. There were a couple times when he would start hitting Nicky to the point where I'd have to jump in between them," Emma recalls. "One time I had to literally lie on top of Nicky to prevent Danny from hitting him anymore. I knew this was not my Danny that was doing this to his son."

This was just one sign of the change beginning to take place in Danny, who was beginning to act like a mobster. He got used to getting things done the way he wanted or else, and on his own timeline. He also got used to people around him fearing him but keeping it under the surface because of his connections. Danny felt powerful having the friends he had. He was tied to and respected by people who could literally make someone disappear. And not only did Danny know it, the people around him had begun to know it too.

Emma remembers that one day Danny came home and was talking about a customer who had come in with an issue of *Life Magazine* from 1969.[28] In it was an article that discussed the Chicago Outfit's ties to Vegas, the Feds' wiretapping of known Mobsters, murder, links to Joe Kennedy, and right at the start of the article were images of Felix Alderisio and Sam Giancana.

"The customer told Danny there was no way he could do business with him anymore, until he separated from those guys," Emma recalls. "The man placed the issue on the desk and walked out the door."

Danny laughed about it at the time, but that small event signaled an end to what they had known before International Fiberglass. Danny had gone from being a small-time but ambitious entrepreneur whose talents led him to contracts with local zoos installing new plastic animal molding machines designed in-part by

---

28   Smith, Sandy. "The Mob. Eavesdropped Conversations." *Life Magazine*, May, 1969.
     http://books.google.com/books?id=a08EAAAAMBAJ&printsec=frontc
     over&source=gbs_ge_summary_r&cad=0#v=onepage&q&f=false

Danny (which are still used today), as well as contracts with Kawasaki motorcycles for a new faring design, to quite simply a Mob associate. The legitimate business was now second in Danny's priorities. Money now came first.

Along with Alderisio's mentoring, Joey Lombardo's involvement with the company had also helped to take Danny to the next level, and the two had become very close in the beginning.

Emma recalls, "Alderisio had brought in Joey [Lombardo] and placed him in a foreman's role within the company, while utilizing Danny's knowledge of the fiberglass industry."

The "foreman" role was simply a front, and even Emma knew this because of how little Joey was ever present at the company doing any actual work. Lombardo's closeness to Danny grew stronger, to the point where Danny and Emma would name their son after him in May of 1970. Unofficially, Lombardo was at that time considered the godfather of Joey Seifert.

Emma recalls, "When Joey was born, Danny gave me the options of Felix, Irwin, or Joey to name him, out of respect for his partners. Quite frankly, I certainly didn't want Felix or Irwin, so Joey he became. At that time, I didn't know Lombardo was actually a Capo for the Mob and helped to run the skim money from the Outfit's interests in Las Vegas. I would find all of this out a couple years later once the FBI approached Danny. My husband would later tell the police that after Lombardo was brought in and the business grew, 'many strange faces started turning up as employees, and the payroll became astronomical.'"

Danny realized that there were things going on in International that even he didn't know about. But it was easy for someone like Danny to self-deceive himself to stay on the right side of the Mob. In reality, the increases in International's payroll were to be expected. They were part of the bigger plan. As long as Danny was highly paid and his partners were happy, he was fine with the situation. As time passed however, things began to change more rapidly for Danny once Alderisio was convicted for bank fraud.

Danny knew that he was losing control over the company. His partners were bringing in people he didn't know or trust. Once Alderisio went to prison in 1970, Danny had very little direct interaction with the operations of the company: he was now a figure-head, being used by the very gangsters to whom he had become intricately tied.

After the death of "Milwaukee Phil" in 1971, Emma remembers her husband changing even more. "Whenever I asked Danny about his business partners, I was told 'the less you know the better off you are.' It became increasingly clear that Danny didn't trust these people—the same people we had considered our friends, and even extended family."

Danny had lost control of his company, and began to feel threatened by his former partners and the new leadership taking over for Alderisio.

It would be three years later in early 1974 that Joey Lombardo, hit-man Anthony Spilotro, and Teamsters leader Allen Dorfman all came under indictment for defrauding the Teamsters Central States Pension Funds of over $1.4 million. For years, the Feds had been looking at International Fiberglass as the vehicle through which the Mob funneled their illegal funds, and the Mob knew it. The gangsters would laugh as they spotted FBI agents conspicuously sitting in sedans across from the factory. The feds would sometimes take pictures of the partners entering or leaving the premises, while the Mobsters would flip the opportunistic "bird" to the Feds' cameras. It became a big game of cat and mouse to both the Feds and Danny's associates.

However, the Mob also knew the Feds would approach Seifert to become a witness; it was only a matter of time. In reality, there was no other option for them. There was no way the Feds could seriously push Lombardo, Weiner, or anyone else involved that had extensive records or influence in the Chicago justice system. They were too powerful and wouldn't crack. Seifert was the weak link as far as the Feds were concerned, and that was something the Mob knew as well.

Danny's choices would have unforeseen consequences far beyond the scope of his own interactions with the gangsters, and would prove to affect the lives of his wife and children for decades. It would all appear inevitable to someone peering from the outside at the past, but this dead-end risk was all simply a gamble on the part of a street kid; and one that paid off handsomely in the short-term for Danny.

Some might also argue that Danny had limited choices in his life; that he was damaged goods, fallen from the start with his upbringing by his own racketeer father and the criminal examples of his brothers. Danny Seifert's family path found him hard-placed in a situation where, because of his ambition, he had painted himself richer but sadder, and into a corner. He did this in the pursuance of what he knew best, fiberglass, and what he thought would prove the best financial route for his family. His motivation may have been selfish on the level of his obsessive need to be a success, but it did include his caring deeply about providing for his own family. He had received little or no direction as a child, and was forced to fend for himself as a very young man. When one is forced to fight in the tough Chicago environment for survival, that individual will be induced or forced to make choices that would seem unacceptable to those people whose middle-class situations simply obliviate the hard choice to do whatever it takes.

The death of Alderisio forced Danny's hand, as those who surrounded him began to lose respect in their interactions with him. He was no longer protected. No one, not even Emma had yet realized that the Feds had approached him. Danny began to protest to Lombardo about the amount of money that was flowing to him; Danny felt that he was owed far more, as his own business was covering their laundering and illegal activities. But by then his partners were already through with Danny and had gotten everything that they had needed. The Mob began to view him more as a liability and less as a partner. Lombardo would simply dismiss Danny's income-related questions and try to brush him aside.

Seifert was also growing more concerned that Cerone was in discussions to officially take over for Alderisio. The two didn't like each other, and neither tried to hide it. Even if Jackie Cerone didn't take over as Mob boss, Danny began to think they would simply do away with him. Weiner had very little to do with the business at this time, and never dealt with the day-to-day operations. That was left up to Lombardo, who coordinated all of it. And even Lombardo was beginning to come down harder on Seifert. Yet Danny knew he needed Lombardo to be on his side, at least for the time being. What he couldn't let happen was to be overrun by his partners; he couldn't let them see any weakness. Otherwise they would become like a pack of wolves and prey on that weakness to destroy him.

To demonstrate his control over the situation, Danny began to think more desperately about a strategy. He knew that he needed to speak their language, and to make a statement. He came up with a plan to not only let them know he was not intimidated by them, but also let them know that he was willing and able to fight for himself, his family, and his stake in the company. But this would mean that he had to discuss at least some part of the severity of the situation with Emma. She needed to know some of it, in order to understand the implications. Once again, he kept most of worries from her, giving her only enough information to make her agree with his intentions to take a stand that he felt was the only remaining option.

If someone were to look through the living room window of the Seiferts' townhouse at this time, they would have viewed a scene that could have been straight out of a Norman Rockwell painting: Joe playing with his cars on the living room floor; Nick and Kathy doing homework around the kitchen table; Danny watching TV while enjoying an end-of-the-day drink; and Emma sewing. As with all Mob families, the surface image would have been insignificant. What no one who would be viewing this scene could perceive was that Emma was sewing Danny a ski mask.

Danny had come up with a plan where he would show up at International, walk inside the company and while wearing a ski mask, empty a full clip from his .45 over the heads of his partners. He knew that his partners would realize it was he who did it, which was exactly the point. He wanted them to know that he could hit them whenever he wanted, just like they could hit him. Lowering or raising his line of fire just a few inches would mean the difference between sending a warning, and a lethal hail of bullets. Not only that, he wanted them to also know he was willing to take it to the next level, to the death, if need be. He would refuse to let them intimidate him. To cover the problem of a witness seeing someone buy a ski mask, he asked Emma to sew it for him. But this led to another set of problems. Danny had to reveal to his wife the danger that he increasingly felt he was in.

Emma recalls how "Danny approached it as a big joke. He really thought the act of shooting over the heads of his partners was going to be fun. He felt it would give him some power back, even if only for a short time."

However, Emma was growing fearful. She was a strong woman and fiercely protective, especially where her children were involved. But she realized that a threat to Danny was also most likely an inevitable threat to her and her children. She was torn because she also felt that Danny really had no one else to turn to in these times; she was the only one who could really support him. Not willing to abandon him and conscious of the potential threat to her family, she agreed to his plan no matter how terrifying it seemed.

Shortly thereafter, Danny chose a morning, walked inside the plant and emptied the .45 as planned. He exited the building and then returned within minutes. His stunned partners stared at him as Danny walked back into the factory and calmly asked, "Who was that guy that just brushed up against my shoulder when I walked in?"

He made it a point to look directly at each of them as he asked, smiling. Danny's tactics did work for a time, and the results were two-fold: they backed off muscling him at work, which allowed him to concentrate on his business. But he'd also planted the seed that allowed him to see the inevitable. He needed to leave International. The question of when to leave would be answered for him when the Feds would approach him one morning at his favorite breakfast place. Like his father before him, he was approached by both the FBI and the IRS. They had evidence, they had motive, and they were looking for him to be the link to their case. Not cooperating posed the threat of going to prison for a long time, hence they tried to force his hand and make him cooperate to be the key witness in bringing down his powerful partners. However, Danny was not ready to roll over for anyone at this point, including the Mob or the Feds. He had his own plans on how next to proceed.

Danny knew that he had proven himself to Lombardo, and decided that he still had some leeway to maneuver. If anything, the stunt with shooting the gun in the factory probably made the Mobsters think he was more on their side rather than the Feds. He also didn't believe that the Feds actually had enough real evidence to convict him; at least not yet. Danny also knew that since he was still involved with the business, it was only a matter of time until his partners got wind of the Feds' approaching him. This meant that he needed to make the first move fast, and play it so that he came across as helping the Mob, while at the same time covering his own ass. He called Lombardo and set up a meeting.

Discussing the evidence that the Feds hinted to him, he told Lombardo that there must only be one way out for the partnership. He knew that this disclosure would put him square on their radar, but he felt he had no choice. He had to try to get rid of any evidence and still prove himself to the Mob, in order to buy time and potentially save his life. Danny felt it was only a matter of time till his Mob partners would become suspicious of his loyalty to them. The Mob would need assurance that he wouldn't talk.

With Lombardo's help, Danny planned on the largest gamble yet—to burn International to the ground. This would destroy any evidence that the Feds had not yet collected, prove his loyalty to his remaining partners, and also allow him to exit the partnership and move on alone in his own direction away from the Mob, the corruption, and the mounting danger. After discussing the details of the plan, Lombardo was convinced and got on board. International would burn.

CHAPTER 8

Burn

The one thing Danny had going for him was that his partners were also on the hook with the Feds. His street smarts made him realize that he would be in a unique bargaining position, even if only briefly. He knew that if he brought the information to his partners, they would think he was on their side since he was looking to destroy evidence. Even though he knew the Mob would suspect him, Danny felt that by playing their game it would buy him some time and potentially destroy enough evidence to keep him from going to prison. He felt it was only a matter of time until the

Feds raided the business, so Danny felt that he knew what he had to do.

When Danny had given his plan to Lombardo, he informed Lombardo that the FBI was looking to bring down everyone in the company. Danny thought that if they burned down the factory, the Feds would only have the evidence that they currently possessed, some of which they had presented to him. He also felt that this evidence most likely wasn't enough to convict him or his partners. In addition, his partners had the local authorities on their payroll and they knew nothing would come of the fire in the way of charges. Once Lombardo had agreed and presented the arson plan to the other partners, they all knew that time was short and everyone got on board with it.

Danny had also sensed the coming of ongoing trouble. Even after burning down International, he and his family would still be at risk from the Mob, who still wanted to ensure Danny's silence by getting rid of him.

"He had long ago taught me how to shoot so I could protect the children and myself, if it ever came to that point," Emma recalls. "I have to admit it was intoxicating. I felt powerful while shooting the gun, like I could protect my family. As things got worse, he took me to the range more frequently to practice. Without hesitation, I know I would have used a gun to defend Danny or the children."

Danny came to understand that he needed to get out of International, whether he wanted to cooperate with the Feds or not. But with his name on the company and the start-up funds having come from Mobsters under Federal investigation, this would be easier said than done. He knew what he had gotten himself into and precisely with whom, and he also knew that he was the easiest Federal target.

In reality, he wanted to get away from Lombardo and the others for the sake of himself and his family. Yet he also wanted to make it loud and clear to both the Feds and the Mobsters that he would not be pushed around. As pissed off as he was at his partners, he was also pissed off at the Feds and knew he was being backed into a corner; a desperate place for anyone, especially Danny.

On a rare, quiet evening at home, Danny told Emma that he was going to leave the company and that he was going to send them all a message. At this point, she had her suspicions but still was quite in the dark as far as Danny's specific plans, which he continued to keep from her for her safety's sake.

"How can you walk away from those men?" Emma remembers asking him.

"I was afraid for Danny, and afraid for our family. I knew that Danny leaving would be difficult enough, but I didn't want him to provoke these men anymore. He promised me that he would leave on good terms with Lombardo; that he had something worked out. But deep down, I sensed otherwise."

Danny left International Fiberglass in December of 1972. In February of 1973, the local papers reported that International Fiberglass had mysteriously burned to the ground[29] the previous night. That day, Danny took his family for a drive in their car and stopped at the charred remains of his company.

His son Nick recalls, "I remember my dad sitting in the car with all of us, silent. He looked at the burned-out building and then started laughing. Mom just stared him as he kept laughing and then pulled away. Joe and I sat quietly in the back seat and we didn't dare say a word. I can still remember seeing my favorite bike leaning against the wall, blackened from the fire. For me, that image signified the end of my childhood because after that point, I was never able to really be a kid anymore. My father slid into his survival mode as my parents tried to protect us and I began to watch after Joe more and more. Little did I know that it would only be just over a year from then till he would be killed."

Unfortunately, Danny's plan of burning the company down to send a message to the Mob and also take care of any evidence that the FBI was trying to use against him, didn't work in either case. Even though Lombardo was involved in the fire, the Mob leadership

---

[29] "Illinois Police and Sheriff's News." *Organized Crime and Political Corruption*. 2006.

was still unhappy with Danny being a liability, and in their minds he was a loose cannon. They decided that they needed assurance Danny would not talk. This assurance would have to come from the person to whom he was closest: Lombardo. And it was reported from inside sources that the word came straight from the top, Tony Accardo himself.

Not long after the fire, International began operating out of a different location. Danny had forfeited his ownership of International to cover his share of the start-up costs in an effort to appease his former associates and show his intentions to honor the business arrangements. Even with the forfeiture, Lombardo tried to squeeze Danny for money to allow him to leave. Danny would have none of it. Deep down, he knew that giving up his share clean and clear would only make them more suspicious of his motives. Lombardo eventually relented and Danny walked away from International, but the Mob was still unsatisfied that he could be trusted.

What no one knew, not even Emma, was that on May 9, 1973, Danny had spoken to IRS investigators and given them an affidavit regarding his involvement in illegal funds linked to International Fiberglass. In this affidavit, he offered them insights into how the Mob would funnel their illegal funds and also detailed the working hierarchy of the leadership in International:

Figure 1. Family Image – Daniel and Emma's Wedding Day

Figure 2. Family Image – Daniel and Emma's Wedding Day
(Irwin Weiner pictured in left corner)

Figure 3. Family Image – Daniel with His Son Joey Seifert (November, 1972)

Figure 4. Family Image – A Young Joey Seifert

Figure 5. Family Image – The Seifert Family

Figure 6. Family Image – The Seifert Family

114

Figure 7. Family Image – Joey and Nick (on the motorcycle Emma saved for)

Figure 8. Family Image – Daniel R. Seifert

Figure 9. Family Image – Joey (left) and Nick (right) at Daniel's grave, 2008

Figure 10. Family Image – Daniel's grave

MEMORIAL HOSPITAL OF DU PAGE COUNTY
Elmhurst, Illinois

REPORT OF POSTMORTEM EXAMINATION

CORONER'S CASE

Name: SEIFERT, DANIEL R. Age: 29 Sex: M Lab.No. A-128-74

Date of death: 9/27/74 Date of admission: DOA

Date of autopsy: 9/28/74 Hospital No. --

Marital status: M Race: W Occupation: Owner of a plastics factory

Place of autopsy: Memorial Hospital of DuPage County

Case doctors: Coroner Matthews Those attending: Coroner

Pathologist H. Dolz, M.D.

FINAL DIAGNOSIS:

1. Multiple shotgun wounds to head with extensive laceration and hemorrhage of brain.
2. Close range shotgun wound of left side of neck with extensive fracture of mandible.
3. Multiple lacerations of scalp, occipital area, caused by blows with blunt object (gun butt).

H. Dolz, M.D.
Pathologist

HD:vs

RECEIVED
DEC - 9 1974

193624

GOVERNMENT EXHIBIT
SEIFERT 29

Figure 11. Family Secrets Trial – Government Exhibit #29 (Coroner's Report)

GROSS EXAMINATION

External Examination

The body is that of a well developed, well nourished, white male measuring 183 cm., weighing approximately 170 lbs. The head is covered with brown hair. The pupils are round and equal, each measuring 0.3 cm. in diameter. The ears and nose are not remarkable except for some blood in both nostrils. In the center of the forehead, about 3.5 cm. above the root of the nose, there is a large roughly triangular skin defect with extensive fracture and opening of the skull bone measuring 5.5 cm. in length and up to 1.2 cm. in diameter. The wound runs into the hairline for a distance of 2 cm. There appears to be a round area of contusion around the lower angle of the wound with an area of excoriation or contusion adjacent to it 1 x 0.3 cm. in diameter. The left temporal - parietal area 7 cm. above the ear shows an irregular rounded wound, probably an entrance wound 1.3 cm. in diameter. Posterior to this wound the skin of the scalp displays numerous irregular, sometimes triangular, lacerations which are grouped in one area about 8 cm. in maximum diameter. They measure up to 3 cm. in length. There are a total of 7 such lacerations. Also areas of hematoma and bruising are scattered between these areas. Immediately proximal to the tragus of the left ear, there is a rounded irregular wound showing contusion of the edges and splitting of the medial skin edges. It measures 1 cm. in diameter and probably represents an entrance wound. Below the left ear, and immediately beneath the left mandibular angle, there is a large irregular wound of "cookie-cutter" appearance 5 x 3 cm. There is extensive laceration of skin and subcutaneous tissue and associated fracture of the mandibular ramus. This wound is surrounded by a large halo of pinpoint and confluent superficial hemorrhages suggestive of powder burns. Above the right eyebrow, there is a roughly triangular laceration 1.5 cm. in maximum diameter. It leaves a rounded area of skin intact which at its lower angle measures 0.5 cm. in diameter. Beneath the right ear is a soft tissue swelling and hematoma associated with multiple small irregular lacerated wounds scattered over an area of 8 cm. and involving the right mandibular area. There are approximately 5 such wounds which measure from 0.5 to 1.2 cm. in diameter and may represent shotgun pellet exit wounds. There is one large such wound immediately above a smaller wound as just described, and this one measures 1.2 cm. in diameter and according to police, a metallic projectile was recovered from this area. There is apparently extensive fracture of both mandibular arches.

The chest is symmetrical. The abdomen is flat. External genitalia and extremities are not remarkable.

Figure 12. Family Secrets Trial – Government Exhibit #29 (Coroner's Report)

REPORT OF POSTMORTEM EXAMINATION

Page 3

A-128-74

Internal Examination

There is no free fluid. Pericardial sac contains the normal amount of fluid. There are a few adhesions of the left base of the lung to the diaphragmatic aspect of the pleura. There are no pulmonary emboli. Also the right lower lobe is partly adherent to the diaphragmatic aspect of the pleura by fibrous adhesions.

Heart: The heart weighs 300 grams. The epicardium is smooth and glistening. There is a normal amount of epicardial fat tissue. The left ventricle measures 1.5 cm. in thickness. The right 0.3 cm. The valves are functional, within normal limits. The coronary arteries are thin-walled and widely patent.

Lungs: The lungs have a combined weight of 800 grams. They are purplish pink, soft, flarly well aerated. There is no bronchial obstruction. A small amount of anthracosis is noted. The pulmonary arteries are not remarkable. The cut surface is purplish tan, somewhat moist with blood.

Liver: The liver is tan brown and weighs 1330 grams. The capsule is smooth. The cut surface is tan brown, moist with blood. The lobular architecture is indistinct. The gallbladder is normal.

Spleen: The spleen is purplish pink, weighs 110 grams. Cut surface is pink. Follicles are indistinct.

Kidneys: The kidneys are normal in size, weight, and shape. They weigh 350 grams combined. The capsule strips with ease. There are no lesions. Ureters and urinary bladder are not remarkable. Prostate is normal in size, weight and shape.

Adrenal glands: Normal.

Pancreas: Normal.

Upper and Lower Gastrointestinal Tract: Show no lesion.

Skull: Upon deflecting the scalp, there is extensive fracture of the frontal and left parietal bones, partially following or approximating the suture lines. There is a punched-out, rounded defect related to the previously described wound above the left ear. Also an irregular defect is seen beneath the wound of the forehead. Related is a large irregular wound in the dura in midline with some hemorrhagic brain tissue escaping from it. A left temporal-parietal laceration of the brain with defect of the dura 3 cm. in diameter is noted.

Figure 13. Family Secrets Trial – Government Exhibit #29 (Coroner's Report)

A-128-74

Skull (Continued):

This is again related to the wound described as at a distance of 5 cm. above the left ear. In the posterior midline, the brain shows an irregular defect in the dura 1.5 cm. in length. A ragged metallic fragment 0.5 cm. in diameter is removed from this area. The entrance wound immediately anterior to the left ear connects to a projectile tract partially destroying the left petrous bone, the left occipital lobe of the brain, and the left cerebellar lobe. A projectile fragment is embedded in the occipital bone causing a depressed fracture 1.5 cm. in diameter. The wound described of the forehead appears to have been inflicted by a projectile passing through the skull at a downward angle and entering adjacent to the crista galli. The projectile which entered the left temporal area and caused a punched-out rounded defect in the left temporal-parietal bone with multiple fracture lines running from it, has penetrated the brain in the left frontoparietal area and a metal projectile, markedly deformed, 1 cm. in diameter is discovered at the base of the brain. A third metal projectile is extracted from immediately beneath the dura overlying the right occipital lobe 2 cm. to the right of the sylvian tissue. There is marked cerebral edema and subarachnoid hemorrhage overlying both occipital lobes, cerebellum and base of the brain. A fourth metal projectile is found in the right posterior neck beneath the right mastoid bone. It measures 1 cm. in diameter. The large blast wound beneath the left ear seems to connect with the exit wound described in the right mandibular area.

H. Dols, M.D.
Pathologist

HD:vs
D-9/28/74
T-9/30/74

Figure 14. Family Secrets Trial – Government Exhibit #29 (Coroner's Report)

REPORT OF POSTMORTEM EXAMINATION

Page 5

A-128-74

MICROSCOPIC EXAMINATION

Heart: Within normal limits.

Lungs: There is some acute passive congestion.

Liver: Minimal fatty change and portal infiltration by lymphocytes.

COMMENT:

There are some discrepancies in this case and it is not entirely possible to reconcile the injuries received with the stories of eye-witnesses and the results of police search.

Any of the injuries to the head and neck are considered of lethal potential except possibly the one in the forehead midline. Only the wound in the left neck can be definitely identified as caused by close range shotgun blast. The other wounds could have been caused by gunshot or pellets from shotgun. The fact that only shotgun shell cases were found at the scene would favor the assumption that the wounds originated from large shotgun pellets. Also the ballistics experts feel that the metal projectiles recovered are consistent with shotgun pellets (buckshot).

H. Dols, M.D.
Pathologist

HD:vs
D-12/5/74
T-12/5/74

Figure 15. Family Secrets Trial – Government Exhibit #29 (Coroner's Report)

121

Figure 16. Family Secrets Trial – Daniel's Body at Crime Scene

Figure 17. Family Secrets Trial – Government Exhibit #8A
(Daniel's body at crime scene)

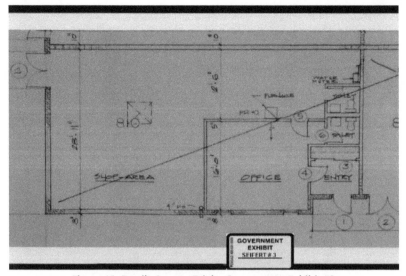

**Figure 18. Family Secrets Trial – Government Exhibit #3
(blueprint of Plasti-Matic Products office)**

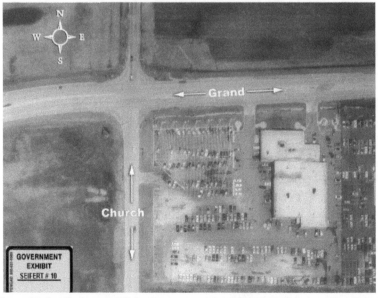

**Figure 19. Family Secrets Trial – Government Exhibit #10, Aerial view, Grand Ave.
and Church Road, Elmhurst, IL (car dealer where one of the getaway cars was found)**

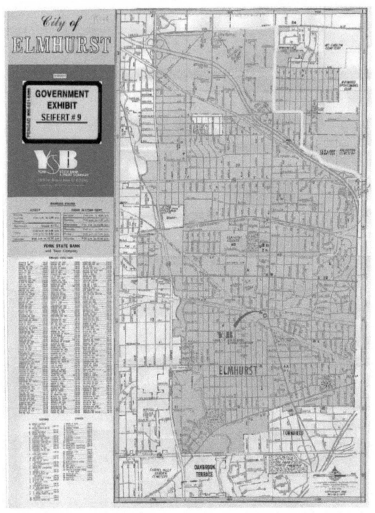

Figure 20. Family Secrets Trial – Government Exhibit #9 (path of car chase)

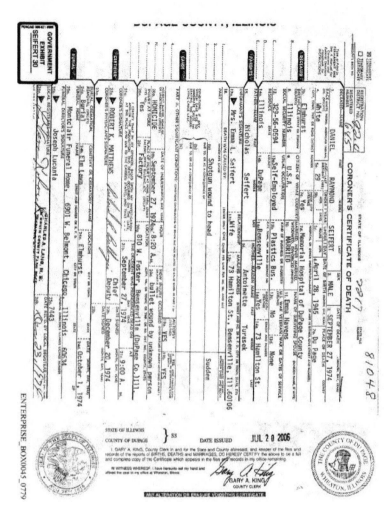

Figure 21. Family Secrets Trial – Government Exhibit #30
(Daniel Seifert's death certificate)

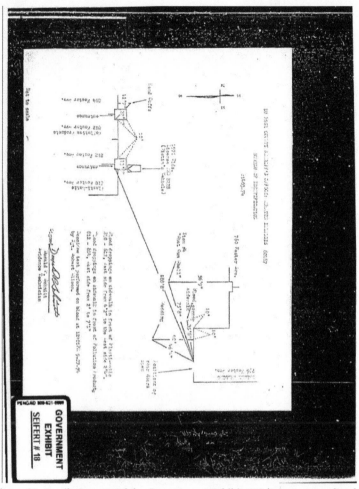

Figure 22. Family Secrets Trial – Government Exhibit #18 (crime scene sketch)

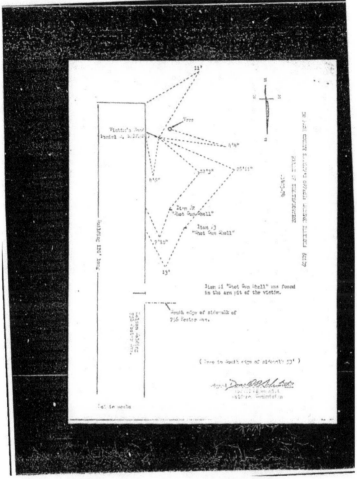

Figure 23. Family Secrets Trial – Government Exhibit #18 (crime scene sketch)

Figure 24. Family Secrets Trial – Government Exhibit #4 (front door of Plasti-Matics)

Figure 25. Family Secrets Trial – Government Exhibit #5 (bloody vacuum cleaner)

JULY 27, 1998

ATTN: Thomas Bourghois

I am sending you this letter in total confidentiality.
IT is very important that you show or talk to nobody
about this letter except who you have to. The less people
that know I am contacting you the more I can and will help
And be able to help you. What I am getting at is I want
to help you and the GOVT. I need for you and only you to
come out to MILAN FCI and we can talk face to face.
NOBODY not even my lawyers know I am sending you this
letter, it is better that way for my safety. Hopefully
we can come to an agreement when and if you choose to
COME HERE. Please if you decide to come make sure very
few staff at MILAN know your reason for coming because
if they do they might tell my father and that would be
a danger to me. The best days to come would be TUES.
OR WEDS. Please no recordings of any kind just bring
pen and lots of paper. This is no game. Ifeel I have to
help you keep this sick man locked up forever.

FRANK CALABRESE JR.
06738-424 inmate #
UNIT G-Right
FCI MILAN MICHIGAN

**Figure 26. Family Secrets Trial – Government Exhibit #1
(letter from Frank Calabrese Jr. to Thomas Bourghois [sic], dated July 27, 1998)**

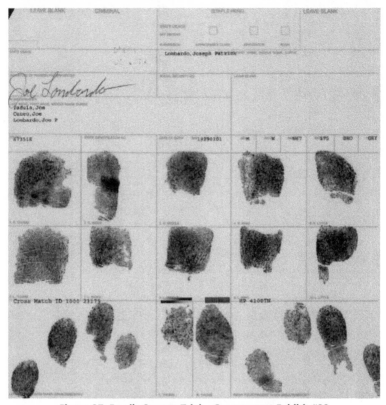

Figure 27. Family Secrets Trial – Government Exhibit #22
(fingerprints of Joey "the Clown" Lombardo)

130

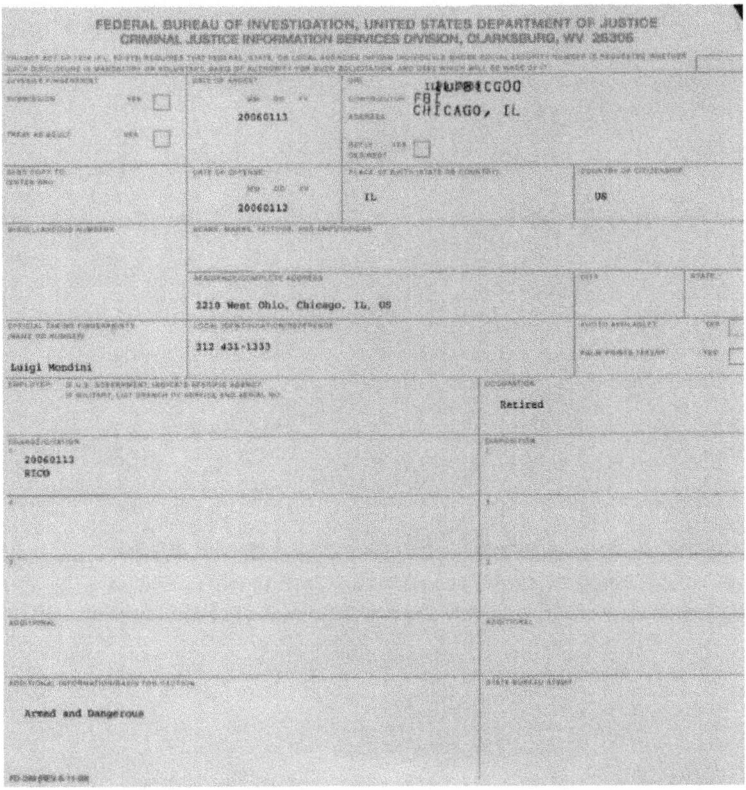

FEDERAL BUREAU OF INVESTIGATION, UNITED STATES DEPARTMENT OF JUSTICE
CRIMINAL JUSTICE INFORMATION SERVICES DIVISION, CLARKSBURG, WV 26306

20060113

[illegible]CG00
FBI
CHICAGO, IL

20060113

IL

US

2210 West Ohio, Chicago, IL, US

312 431-1333

Luigi Mondini

Retired

20060113
RICO

Armed and Dangerous

Figure 28. Family Secrets Trial – Government Exhibit #22 (fingerprints of Joey "the Clown" Lombardo)

Figure 29. Family Secrets Trial – Government Exhibit #2
(aerial view of office complex where Plasti-Matic Products was located)

Figure 30. Family Secrets Trial – Government Exhibit #28
(witness' car damaged during getaway)

Figure 31. Family Secrets Trial – Government Exhibit #7
(getaway car found in car dealer lot)

Figure 32. Family Secrets Trial – Government Exhibit #13
(flip-down license plate holder)

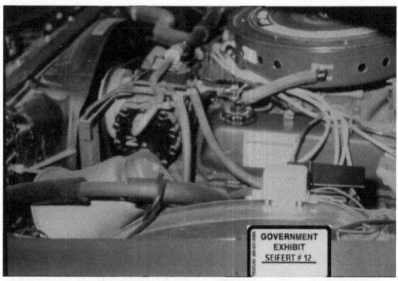

Figure 33. Family Secrets Trial – Government Exhibit #12 (motor of getaway car)

Figure 34. Family Secrets Trial – Government Exhibit #14A
(kill switches for lights used in getaway car)

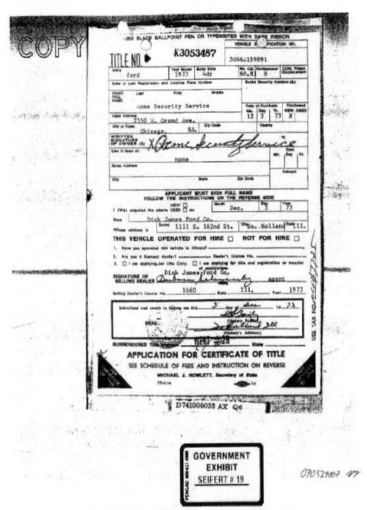

Figure 35. Family Secrets Trial – Government Exhibit #19
(title of car used as one of the getaway cars)

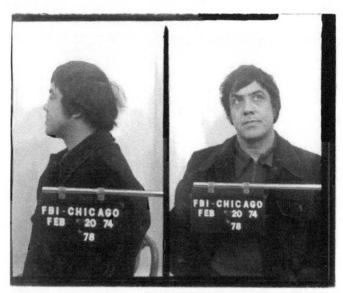

Figure 36. Family Secrets Trial – Government Photo Array
(mugshot of Joey "the Clown" Lombardo)

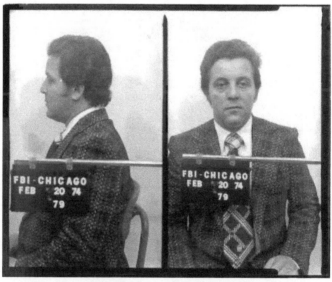

Figure 37. Family Secrets Trial – Government Photo Array
(mugshot of Tony "the Ant" Spilotro)

Figure 38. Family Secrets Trial – Government Exhibit #52 (Irwin Weiner)

Figure 39. Family Secrets Trial – Government Exhibit #3
(Felix "Milwaukee Phil) Alderisio)

**Figure 40. Family Secrets Trial – Government Exhibit #15
(Jackie "the Lackey" Cerone)**

**Figure 41. Family Secrets Trial – Government Exhibit #48
(Frank "the German" Schweihs)**

Figure 42. Family Secrets Trial – Government Exhibit #54 (Allen Dorfman)

Figure 43. Family Secrets Trial – Government Exhibit #81 (Frank Calabrese Jr.)

Figure 44. Family Secrets Trial – Government Exhibit #1
(the "Last Supper" photo with Anthony Accardo, Joseph Aiuppa, Dominic Di Bella, Vincent Solano, Alfred Pilotto, Jackie Cerone, Joseph Lombardo, James Torello, Joseph DiVarco, and Joseph Amato)

I was formerly president of International Fiberglass Inc. (an Illinois Corp.), resigned effect [sic] December 1972 (just before X-mas). Within 30 days prior to 10/6/1971 Joe Lombardo approached me and told me that "we got a check coming into International Fiberglass. Let me know when it comes in." I had no knowledge of what reason we would receive a check unless it was for business purposes. The check came in from Gaylord [sic] Products on 10/6/1971 (#10013) issued to International Fiberglass drawn on the Michigan Avenue National Bank of Chicago. I deposited the $5250 check into the International Fiberglass checking account at the Bensenville State Bank.

Joe Lombardo came back to me and directed me to issue checks for the same amount of money we received from Gaylord Products Inc. I issued two checks, #740 dated 10/9/71 for #1,000.00 and #754 dated 10/16/71 for $4250.00 to Joe Lombardo allegedly for back wages.

I had no knowledge as to the reason Gaylord [sic] Products Inc. issued the check to International Fiberglass. There was no purchase of material or the sale of material (or merchandise) by International Fiberglass from Gaylord [sic] Products Inc.

Joe Lombardo directed me to issue an invoice in October 1972, to Gaylord [sic] Products Inc. for vacuum forming dies to cover the check for $5250 we received on or about 10/6/71 (and subsequently paid out to Joe Lombardo).

Joe Lombardo was in charge of operations of International Fiberglass, even though I had the title "President." Lombardo worked under the direction of Irwin Weiner who told Lombardo he represents us stockholders.

If Joe Lombardo directed me to do something I would have to follow his orders because he (Lombardo) would remind me that he represented the stockholders; he did not represent me, only Weiner, Harold Lurie, and Micky Caplan.

After leaving International, Danny worked for about a month at his uncle's steel company, but his uncle got spooked when the Mob came around looking for Danny. So Danny left and then started his own fiberglass company called "Plasti-Matic Products" in Bensenville, Illinois. This time, his only partner would be his wife, Emma.

Lombardo, through directives from above, began using scare tactics against Danny and his family to make sure he wouldn't talk. The Mob was growing increasingly uneasy about Danny. Lombardo was an expert at such pressuring tactics, and knew the subtle ways to make his point. He began to simply make his presence felt, such as frequently driving by the Seiferts' house, sitting in a car down the street from their house, and making threatening phone calls at different times of the day.

Nick recalls one day he was riding his bike when he saw Lombardo sitting in a car down the street. He rode his bike up to him as always and asked why he was sitting there.

"Lombardo replied that he was just waiting for [Nick's] dad, and that he'd go inside in a little bit," Nick remembers. "When my dad came home a little later, I went into the kitchen and didn't see Lombardo. I asked him, 'where's Uncle Joey?' My dad looked at me and questioned why I had been asking. I told him that I saw him in a car down the street and talked to him. This made dad grab his gun and move us all downstairs while he looked outside and made sure no one was around. I obviously didn't know what was really going on, but I knew enough to realize that something was wrong, and that Uncle Joey was somehow involved."

At this point, the FBI already had all the evidence they needed, so the pressure for Seifert to cooperate only intensified. It became clear to him that his only choices were either going to prison to stay in the good graces of the Mob, at least for the time being, or cooperating with the Feds and getting to stay with his family. Lombardo approached Danny one day and told him that the bosses suggested he do the time. Lombardo told him that they'd take care of his family while he was in prison and once he was out, they'd have him work for Cerone. He'd have to have very little contact with Lombardo, but he and his family would be well-taken care of.

Danny didn't buy it. While he didn't completely trust the Feds, he trusted his former associates even less and felt the Mob would certainly have him killed in prison. He knew the Mob would never allow loose ends. His mind was made up. Danny flipped and offered his services to the Feds in a last-ditch effort to protect himself and his family. This led to the official indictments by the Feds against his former partners in early 1974.

"Danny had decided to cooperate with the FBI and he introduced me to several agents that he began working with," Emma recalls. "I was told by them not to worry, because they didn't think anything would happen. Then, there were several more attempts at scare tactics again; phone calls and drive-bys."

Danny became increasingly paranoid after the indictments, which began to affect his marriage.

"We tried to have a normal life but I don't think anything was normal except for the emotional support that my family always gave us. In 1974, my relationship with Danny had become very strained. I thought once he testified, everything might be better. I was so tired; I was just resigned to whatever might happen."

But there was no way that Emma could have imagined the brutal murder that the Mob had planned for her husband. Everything was on the line for these Mobsters. Danny, as a key witness for the prosecution, was not only a major threat to tens of millions of dollars ready for the Mob's taking, but his testimony could also ensure hard prison time for his former associates.

Emma remembers having premonitions close to the time of the killing, sensing something terrible was coming. "A week before he was killed, Lombardo and his girlfriend Bonnie Vent, came to the factory to talk to Danny about some problems with the wax that was used in the [fiberglass] production process. When Danny came home, he told me that he felt like Joey wanted to discuss something with him, but never actually got around to it."

"Several days later, I had an eerie feeling that this wasn't going to end well because I had come downstairs and found Danny sleeping on the couch. He was positioned just like he would have been in a coffin. I also had a dream about the day of the murder, but because of how bad the dream was, I forced myself to forget it. Had I only remembered, perhaps things would have been different; maybe I could have changed it."

To this day, Emma laments not discussing that dream with her husband. Yet she knows that there would be no stopping Danny. One of his last comments to her regarding his role in the trial was, "This is my last chance to make a splash." If Danny was going down in any way, he was going to take as many of them with him as possible, legally or lethally. It didn't matter to him at that point which way they wanted to go about it.

Danny's murder on September 27, 1974 would have complex effects on multiple facets of his family's lives. First, with Danny gone, all the weight of testimony would fall upon the shoulders of another associate involved with International, Harold Lurie, who was not made of the same tough mettle as Danny. The Feds had gotten to Lurie too, and with Seifert gone, their whole case rested on what Lurie would say in court. But the Mob knew they could intimidate Lurie far easier than Seifert, and with such a violent, well-broadcast murder such as Seifert's, Lurie would think twice before talking on the stand.

At the start of the trial, Lurie performed ineptly as expected by the Mob, and quickly crumbled. Suddenly he couldn't remember a thing and the case fell apart for the prosecution. The men who were responsible for Danny's murder walked out of court with all charges relating to the Teamsters fraud dropped. For Emma, Joe, and Nick, it would be 33 years to the day of Danny's murder before any of the men responsible would be brought to justice.

Several days after the murder, Emma received a hand-written note, with no signature or return address. These were not needed; she knew it was from Harold Lurie. The note read:

My heart goes out to you and your family. A sincere offer of consolation at this time of past terror and deep loss from one who has experienced the same fear, but who admires the strength and integrity your husband exhibited. His work for the authorities may help to eliminate the evil that took his life.

The "strength" that Danny exhibited, as stated in Lurie's note, had not gone unnoticed by the Mob. This was no ordinary hit by any means. Danny, while back at International, was known for his toughness by his partners, who had set up a heavy bag and an area to box with each other to blow off steam. They knew him as a tough guy and street fighter.

Another infamous Mob hit-man, Tony Spilotro, would sometimes come around International as well, to talk to his Capo (or boss), Lombardo. Tony, like Lombardo, was also a boxer as a youth, and Lombardo would always egg him on to fight Danny; but Spilotro never would. He knew how fast Danny was and Danny had the reach over Spilotro, who stood only around 5'6" at best. Spilotro was someone who would never get into a position to let himself get shown up by anyone.

But Danny's true toughness came from within; and paired with his physical fighting abilities the Mob took no chances and had multiple gangsters on the scene that day to make sure the job was done correctly. The Mob was certain that nothing short of death would ever stop Danny from something once he put his mind to it. The same can be said for Danny's sons, who inherited not only his toughness, stubbornness, and entrepreneurship, but also became the unwilling inheritors of the secrecy and harmful effects of that day. Each would spend decades chasing down the answers to questions about their dad's murder that no one either had or no one would give them.

The events that surrounded Danny during those years, including the "terror" that Lurie spoke of, would come to haunt his family throughout their lives. However, it would be Joe and Nick who would be the most affected by the murder. They were young, and the loss festered within them, building each year. As they grew older, the experience would harden into a cold, unmitigated resolve. They would be haunted from within rather than terrorized from the outside such as their father had experienced, but would still be haunted nonetheless. And the premonition that Nick had of a childhood ending when he viewed his charred bicycle, would be far more profound than he could ever imagine.

CHAPTER 9

Evidence

As expected, the investigations that took place after Danny's murder uncovered multiple pieces of evidence that pointed directly to Mob involvement. It was hardly a surprise to anyone given the style and brazenness of the hit, and especially considering who his partners were. When Danny's true evidentiary role in the aborted trial was revealed, it left little doubt for even the most casual observer. But as time went by, corruption became an increasingly evident piece to the puzzle.

As the homicide investigations ensued, things began to emerge that illustrated a well-planned and orchestrated hit on Seifert. For example, a couple days before the murder, investigators discovered that a receptionist who worked in the office complex spotted someone sitting in a car after she almost backed into him. She thought it was quite strange that someone would just be sitting in a car so early in the morning, and she didn't recognize the car to be owned by anyone who worked in the complex, which she would be used to seeing each morning. After going through police photos, the individual whom she almost hit turned out to be none other than John Fecarotta, a known Mob lieutenant who ranked just behind Angelo "the Hook" LaPietra. Fecarotta was one of the three gangsters suspected to be part of the outside crew, which had waited in case Danny was to run outside.

Another witness who came forward was a woman whose car was sideswiped by one of the getaway cars. After looking through photos of suspects, she quickly identified Mob hit-man Tony Spilotro as one of the passengers in the car that hit her.

A third witness, intentionally left unnamed here, was a worker in the company across from Plasti-Matic. He was the only witness to actually see the execution of Danny. He watched as a gunman, not masked, shot Danny in the leg, and then another walked up with a shotgun and shot him point-blank in the head. That gunman then turned and looked at Norton, who wisely turned and ran into the company to hide.

As the gangsters were making their getaway after the hit, there was one piece of evidence that would come out at a later date that would highlight and underscore the theories of corruption and cover-up that surround this case.

Just after the murder, as the getaway cars split up, they were pursued by several police units. All of the fleeing cars eluded the chasing police forces and none were caught. Thirty-five years after the murder, an officer who refuses to give his name or which police unit he worked for at the time, informed the Seiferts at the time of writing this book that he was directly behind one of the cars and was ordered by someone on his police radio to end the pursuit. At the time he replied, "But I have them! They are right in front of me!" However, the commander who was on the radio that morning ordered all of the officers to back off from the chase.

There was never an explanation about the questionable recall, and the person on dispatch was never questioned by any Federal or local authorities about this incident. By coincidence, at the time of the Family Secrets Trial, the officer happened to be in the Federal building for business when he overheard Nick talking to one of the FBI agents. Under the condition of anonymity, the officer approached Nick and told him what happened that morning during the chase. The information is something that he cannot discuss publicly, and it did not come out in the trial, but he felt that "Nick and Joe had a right to know that there were powers behind these guys getting away with their father's murder."

In addition, Joey Lombardo, a prime suspect from the start of any police or FBI investigation was reading an article in the paper about the murder when the police approached him that evening. He of course denied taking any part in it, but decades later, evidence would point otherwise. Several days after the murder, a small-time associate named Alva Johnson overheard Joey Lombardo and Marshall Caifano, another known high-ranking Mobster linked to Alderisio and Alderisio's cousin Louis Fratto, joking about Danny's murder at a local driving range. Johnson stated under oath that he overheard Lombardo say to his associate, "That S.O.B. won't testify now," which is the same expression the main masked intruder used when he demanded to Emma on the morning of the murder, "Where is that S.O.B.," when the gunmen were looking for Danny. Alva Johnson would stick by his story and repeat it to the jury 33 years later in the Family Secrets Trial.

Additionally, one of Lombardo's fingerprints was later identified on the title of a brown 1973 Ford LTD, one of the getaway cars used in the hit. The LTD was found parked in a Mob-connected car dealership in Elmhurst Illinois, not far from the murder scene, and was listed as being owned by Acme Security Service, at 2350 West Grand Avenue in Chicago.[30]

Roy L. McDaniel is one of the FBI investigators who examined evidence from the Seifert murder back in October of 1974. On the car's title, one of the Mobsters signed "Acme Security Services" in the signatory line for the owner. Underneath the "Ser" in the "Acme Security Service" signature was a useable print that McDaniel found during his initial investigation in 1974. In a comparison search, McDaniel matched it positively to one of Lombardo's prints, specifically his left middle finger.

Decades later in 2007, McDaniel would find himself as an expert witness in the Family Secrets trial. By then, he was not only a 40-year veteran of the FBI laboratory, but was also considered an expert on fingerprints and someone who had testified for the FBI over 90 times during his career.

McDaniel stated to the jury of the Family Secrets trial, "All your ten fingers are different from each other. You have them before you are born and you'll have them until you decompose after death. Only one finger of everybody in the world could've made that particular print," McDaniel continued, as an image of Lombardo's print compared to that found on the title was displayed on a large

---

[30] US Department of Justice, Operation Family Secrets
http://www.justice.gov/usao/iln/hot/familySecrets.html#Jul10

screen positioned in the courtroom for the jury. "And that would be the finger of Joey Lombardo."

As for the address of the car, 2350 West Grand Avenue turned out not to be the address for Acme Security Services, but rather for Menotti Plumbing and Heating, owned by one of Lombardo's friends.

Besides a police scanner that investigators found installed in the getaway car, ski masks were found in the trunk of the car that matched Emma's description of the masks worn by the men inside the factory. Inside one of the masks a few hairs were found, which were kept by the police as potential evidence.

Decades later in 2003, FBI agents would surprise Lombardo at a machine shop he worked at almost on a daily basis. Lombardo had always kept busy, and loved to work with his hands. Agents swept in unannounced and swabbed Lombardo's mouth for DNA, to match against the hairs found so many years ago in one of the ski masks. Unfortunately, the time lapse was too long and no DNA was recoverable from the hairs to match the recent swabs.

What the police scanner that was found in the LTD did disclose however, was that it could be traced by its serial number to a sales receipt taken from a local Chicago store, C.B. Center of America. A sales representative named Mark Rokicki, who worked at C.B. Center, was called in 2007 as a witness in the trial. He discussed before the jury how one of his best customers, Advanced

Towing and Services, would come in and pay cash for everything. When he offered them a discount through a credit program, his customers declined, refusing to fill out any paperwork on their company. Rokicki also discovered later that the contact phone number the men gave was a non-working number.

The sales representative described to the jury how whenever the men from Advanced Towing would come into the store to purchase equipment, two other men would come with them and position themselves by the windows as if they were looking out for something. The particular scanner found in the Ford LTD was part of a large single purchase they made with several other items, and Rokicki was able to pick out Joey "the Clown" Lombardo as the man who signed for the goods, using the name "J. Savard."[31]

In addition to all of these pieces of evidence, others would surface that showed an intricate web of planning for the hit. Frank Schweihs, another ruthless hit-man who is suspected of mishandling Danny (who never should have escaped the two men that stormed into the office that morning), had bought over $3,000 worth of police scanning equipment in the weeks before the murder. Evidence would point to Schweihs, Lombardo, LaPietra, and Fecarotta all being part of the purchases and linked to Advanced Towing Services. The name "J. Savard" was used on eight of the

---

[31] US Department of Justice, Operation Family Secrets
   http://www.justice.gov/usao/iln/hot/familySecrets.html#Jul10

invoices, and J. Savard was none other than Schweihs' wife at the time.

Interestingly, in addition to all of the pieces of evidence that would be presented in the trial, Danny had been hassled by the police for weeks before the murder when he was simply driving to work. Seifert family members suspect that corrupt police knew he'd be carrying a gun with him and that by constantly pulling Danny over would make him do one of two things: either not carry his gun, or make Emma hold it for him because he knew the police would never search her for a weapon.

One single point has become a focus for Danny's sons in their search for the truth. They question how it was that the men who entered the office that day were able to get the jump on Danny. Was that for some reason he didn't have a gun with him at that moment, or was it because as he distractedly wrestled with the vacuum cleaner and the hoses, the gangsters were able to surprise and quickly overpower him? No one can say for sure, but in those days Danny never went anywhere without his .45, and Emma recalled seeing him tuck into his waistband that morning. The fact that he was being pulled over multiple times on his way to the office in the weeks leading up to the murder demonstrates to his sons the collusion of "priming" him for the Mob hit by the authorities tied to the Mob. Danny's .45 was also never found after the murder, leading his sons to believe that he must have had it with him that morning.

The recovered getaway cars were all outfitted for surveillance with police scanners and had the modifications that showed they were designed for one purpose—to be Mob getaway cars. They had switches to disable the brake lights, flip down license plates, and steel-reinforced bumpers and panels for ramming into other cars during getaways.[32]

In addition, no one could point to why Danny hadn't been offered the same witness protection plan that Harold Lurie had been offered. Not only that, but the jurors in the trial in which Danny was supposed to be a witness would not be told of Danny's murder, nor would they learn of any testimony involving Alderisio's past Mob involvement prior to his death, nor of the Federal protection afforded to Lurie. All of this suppressed on grounds of prejudice, as argued by the defense. Jurors were also forbidden to read the local Chicago papers out of further fear of prejudice. The defendants had been painted simply as independent businessmen. It was ruled that as long as the defendants didn't testify themselves, the jury could not hear of their backgrounds. The charges against Lombardo were then conveniently dropped by the prosecution after Danny's murder, since Danny was to be the primary witness against him.

To the Seiferts, when they assess all of the facts surrounding all the events of that morning, such as the strange order to pull off

---

[32] US Department of Justice, Operation Family Secrets
http://www.justice.gov/usao/iln/hot/familySecrets.html#Jul10

the police chase, as well as the acquittals that were the result of Danny's murder, the only conclusion that they can draw is conspiracy. The Mob allegedly "owned" many of the police and law enforcement agencies working in the cities that surround Chicago, as well as attorneys and judges (as well-documented in the Operation Greylord case[33] in 1980s Chicago), and it wouldn't take much to ensure that a chase or even a murder ended well for the gangsters. These uncovered pieces of evidence all point to this corruption, which has been the main catalyst for the unending search for the truth on the part of Danny's family, especially his sons.

[33] "Investigation of Public Corruption." Federal Bureau of Investigation, March 2004.
http://www.fbi.gov/news/stories/2004/march/greylord_031504

CHAPTER 10

Emma Survival

Directly after the murder, Emma tried to protect her children by shielding them from as much information as she possibly could. The truth surrounding Danny's murder was bad enough, but the TV stations and most of the reporters made it seem that their father was a full-blown mobster, while at the same time the Mob was labeling him a rat for turning on them. But the effort on Emma's part to shield her children from Danny's now-destroyed life would only prove to later fuel Nick's and Joe's own drives to discover the truth about why their father was killed.

Emma and her children found themselves in a position of complete uncertainty. She had to raise her kids alone, and provide income for her family, and somehow find the strength to endure the pain of losing her husband in such a brutal manner. Above all, they as a family needed to survive. She found herself drawing upon an unknown inner strength within herself, yet also found that she was fragile inside and increasingly vulnerable; something that would not go unnoticed by those who surrounded her.

For the first few days and weeks after Danny's murder, Emma was so focused on keeping everyone else from falling apart she didn't have time to worry about her own emotions and hardships. She kept busy by burying her husband and doing her best to protect and insulate the kids from the media, not to mention keeping tight control over her persistent fear that the Mob's hit-men might come after her or her children. Every stranger or unknown car driving down the block loomed as a possible threat. In addition, even with the money secured from Danny's business's checking account, the discovery of the unsigned life insurance policy made Emma realize that she had very little money to pay for a funeral.

Danny's family had distanced themselves from Emma, and offered no help to defray any of the costs or even assist her with the funeral plans. So, with the blessing from her Aunt, Emma's parents gave her two empty family plots in the same cemetery where her grandparents were buried.

"My family had eight plots altogether, and they gave me two so that Danny and I would be together again someday," Emma recalls. "Ironically, this turned out to be right across the street from where Danny's own father had been buried."

Yet it would be the normal everyday things that most people take for granted, Emma discovered, which would prove to be the hardest tasks for her: a drive by a favorite place that she and Danny had visited together, hearing a song they both liked ("My Way" by Frank Sinatra was one of Danny's favorites), seeing a show on TV that Danny used to enjoy, etc. All of these things seemed to frequently draw her and yet haunt her. Even shopping became a frightening experience for her, since it meant that she needed to be surrounded by potentially harmful strangers.

A day or so before the funeral, Emma could remember going into a Sears store to buy the children some nice shoes. These shoes were not for the new school year that had started a few weeks prior, as other normal parents were shopping for, but for her children to wear to the funeral.

"None of the sales people were helping us," she recalls. "I finally walked up to a young man and told him I hated to cut in front of other people, but my children needed shoes for their father's funeral."

She remembers that the clerk was very compassionate and helped them right away ahead of the other customers that were in line. She then rushed the children out of the store immediately, because she had become paranoid—wary of all the strangers around her. Even today, she still can't tolerate pressing crowds and gets nervous at the sight of closed doors. These are some of the lasting effects Emma suffers, all caused by the residual emotional trauma from the murder.

As the family made final preparations for the funeral and the wake, they gathered together with mixed emotions. On the one hand, there was a deep sadness stemming from the events that had occurred, noticeable especially in the children from the loss of their father. Yet on the other hand, there was a silent sigh of relief that the scary events leading up to this were finally over. Before Danny's murder, Emma's sister Judy had accurately predicted that his cockiness and antagonistic approach to his former partners would end up "knocking him off of his high-horse." But she had assumed he would end up in jail rather than in a coffin.

During these difficult times, Judy had become a reliable pillar of strength for Emma. As the family planned for Danny's services, she once again would demonstrate the fortitude Emma had come to rely on.

"Judy and I went together to the funeral home to make plans for Danny's wake and burial," Emma recalls. "While we were there, two men walked in and started asking us a lot of questions. They didn't show any identification, but announced to us that they were FBI."

The agents took advantage of the weakened state of Emma at that time in order to grill her to see if she could or would divulge any information that she hadn't already given the police.

"At the time, I was just focused on trying to bury my husband and protect my kids. All of a sudden I had two guys asking all these questions, and I can't honestly even remember what all they were asking or how exactly I responded. But after a little bit, it became clear that they were in fact agents, and I gave them the statement they asked for," Emma remembers.

This statement would end up being one of the main arguments that Lombardo's attorney, Rick Halprin, would attempt to use decades later as an argument against her testimony in court, while he attempted to prove inconsistencies in her depositions and testimonies over the years.

Surprising Emma at such a vulnerable time may have been an investigative tactic by the agents, but it was also a dangerous one. What the agents didn't know was that Emma was carrying her gun with her in her purse, and Judy, thinking quickly, clasped her sister's arm as she noticed Emma moving her hand toward the purse.

"I was actually ready to grab the gun for her," Judy recalls of the incident. "We had no idea who these guys were, and at that moment, we were ready for anything, considering all that we had been through. Once we realized who they really were, we were more pissed off at the timing they chose to approach us than anything else. I have no idea how they would expect someone in Emma's situation that day to have the reliable state of mind to give an accurate statement."

Later, at Danny's wake, another strange incident would cause Emma and Judy to question whether or not they were being watched by the men responsible for the murder of her husband.

"We noticed that there was someone walking around that no one knew," Emma remembers of the event. "He didn't know any of us, but was apparently just a weirdo that was interested in observing these types of things. We took no chances. We told him to leave and Judy followed him outside, and watched closely as he went down the alley and out of sight."

Judy remembers, "That guy had no idea I had Emma's gun with me in my pocket as I watched him walk away. I stood there, watching him disappear, feeling the cold metal in my hand. I didn't care; I would have done anything to protect Emma."

After Danny was laid to rest, Emma's family took the children back to her parent's house and Emma privately said her quiet goodbyes to her husband. It was the start of October, the beginning of autumn in Chicago. For Emma, it marked the end of her most frantic time. Yet it would also prove to be the beginning of an ensuing desperate time, one of anger and lingering paranoia.

Part of that rage stemmed from her bitter knowledge that Danny hadn't been better protected by the FBI and the police. He was obviously a pivotal figure in the case and no one could understand why he didn't have a heavy shield of witness protection. It was an unanswerable question, since he had never discussed his position in the case with anyone out of concern for his family's safety. But it was suspected by his family that those around him knew something. Maybe someone had dropped the ball in protecting him, either out of sheer stupidity or perhaps out of some darker and more corrupt motive. Decades later, an anonymous insider would approach Nick and tell him that Danny's Federal handlers had secretly refused any additional protection for him, but by now this could not be proven.

"I remember shortly after his death, there was a newspaper article about the murder with a picture of US District Attorney Jim Thompson talking to someone," Emma recalls. "And the quote read, 'I didn't think he was that important to the case.' I was furious. How could he possibly say they didn't know? Danny was the only one that had crucial inside information. Several years later, I happened to see Jim Thompson, who had by then become the Governor of Illinois, in the airport, and it took all my strength not to go up to him and tell him what I thought of his quote!"

Only two weeks after the murder, Emma knew that she needed to go back to work. She simply had no choice; she and her family needed money and a way to survive. She had to go back to the factory to somehow try to make it all work for her children. She couldn't afford a cleaning service, so she was forced to go in and clean up the murder site after the police had left, by herself. This meant cleaning splatters of her husband's blood off the walls, the carpet, the floor, and then straighten the place up as much as possible to remove traces of the murder and of the ensuing investigation's traffic.

"I've blacked all that out of my mind, and don't really remember much, other than seeing the blood in the entry way. I do know that I was very scared and made sure the inside doors in the office were always open."

Every second inside the factory reminded her of the horror of that day. Yet regardless of the emotional pain it would inflict, she knew that she needed to go and work inside the same office where she witnessed her husband beaten and killed. This was now her company and it was the only source of potential income for her family, and as difficult as it was to be there, she needed to do it. Somehow, she had to try to learn to handle everything that Danny had controlled and done in the company. Even with the help of her family, it was extremely difficult for her.

"I had to get up in the morning, get the three children ready for school, drop them off, and then go to work by myself in that building," she recalls. "I would then pick them up every day from school because I was so scared of something happening to any of them. Then I'd take them home to my parents' house and go back to work in the factory until late at night. I had to do everything there: from the finances, to answering the phone, to the sales, and I'd even be in the back working with the fiberglass to try and get orders out in time."

A few weeks after the murder, Emma was called to testify in a DuPage County Coroner's Inquisition, in order to legally determine the cause of death.

"There I was, still in shock, exhausted, and I had to sit in a chair in front of a panel of ten or twelve people, similar to a Grand Jury, and answer whatever questions they wanted to ask me regarding his death. I remember this vividly, as I purposely wore the same jacket that I had worn the day of Danny's murder. It still had small spots of his blood on it. I think I wore it to have some connection to him, to feel safe in some way, as if he was there with me. It was a terrible experience and just added to the stress of everything during that time."

In the following months, Emma and her children would visit Danny's grave almost every single morning.

"Regardless of how difficult it was, we made the time to get up early enough to make it there before I had to get the kids to school," she recalls. "We needed that at first. I needed that. And the children needed that last connection to their father."

Nick remembers one instance around Christmas of 1974, when the family went to visit Danny's grave. "The three of us saw the sadness in our mom, but as difficult as it was to see his grave, it made us all still feel connected to him. It was as if we could still feel him, even if it was just in our minds. One day we all went to the grave. It was brutally cold and we [the kids] couldn't even stand out there for very long. The wind chill had to be below zero, and was so cold your face felt like it was getting burned. But mom knelt down next to the grave and closed her eyes. She was completely unaffected by the cold. She knelt there, in the snow and cold for what seemed like forever as the three of us sat in the car."

Emma knew this type of grieving couldn't go on for very long, for the sake of the children. "After several months of it, I knew that I needed to end that practice in order to help the children begin to move on. I realized that it was becoming damaging to them on some level, so I told them we would go only on the weekends, to start to wean them off a bit."

Even so, Emma would continue to go to the graveyard on her own and privately visit her husband and talk to him, trying to hold on to her fading memories of him; trying to stay connected. She wanted to sustain the feelings that she knew she would slowly start to lose as the memories of her husband grew fainter.

Reflecting back on this time, Nick remembers, "Somehow, no matter how long of a day she had, from getting us ready for school, going to work, visiting Dad's grave, etc., she always tried to be home in time to tuck us into bed. That lifestyle became the norm for her, and looking back on it as an adult, I have the greatest respect for the strength she had. I honestly don't know how she did it."

The only private time that Emma had to herself was late at night when she would go to bed and sometimes cry herself to sleep. She did her best not to break down in front of the children to not upset them anymore than what they were already suffering through. She didn't allow herself to rest, as the downtime would only cause her to sink deeper into depression. Everything around her reminded her of her husband, and she found herself reflecting on her every step within the relationship. She even questioned when she could have changed the direction or the outcome. Yet she knew dwelling morosely on these thoughts would only drive her crazy, and she did her best to push past them and to focus on what she needed in order to get through that time—her job and raising her children.

As difficult as those days were, there was a hidden blessing that emerged, which was an indescribable closeness that developed between her and her children. "Some of my strongest memories are how much my children and I loved each other and how much I had to fight to keep us together," Emma recalls of that time.

"For me, a breaking point came on a Saturday morning, only a couple weeks after Danny's funeral. I had put the three children in the car and we were driving to the factory because I had to do some work there. I must have been looking especially sad that day, because at a stop light, little Joey leaned over and put his arm around me and told me out of the blue, 'Mommy, I don't think those men meant to hurt my daddy.' There was this little four-year-old kid trying to comfort me, and I just lost it. I hugged him with every part of my soul, and Nick and Kathy then leaned over from the back seat and hugged all of us. A horn honked from behind us and life returned. We continued on."

For the next several weeks, Emma did her best to manage caring for her children, run the company, and trying to mend the slowly shattering pieces of her life. She began to realize that there was probably no way she could continue to run Plasti-Matic Products by herself.

"Danny's brother Bob tried to convince me to let him take Danny's place in the company, but I refused," she recalls. "He would come in sometimes to help, but there was no way I was going to bring him into the company on any sort of ownership level. Weeks before Danny was killed, he happened to mention to me that if anything were ever to happen to him, that I shouldn't let Bob into the company, and not to trust him with the business. Those words rang true for me, and I decided that I'd rather let the company go down than bring him in."

For the time being, Emma struggled on as best she could by herself, taking in what little money she could from the business, and still doing her best to move emotionally forward from Danny's death. Every day she felt and lived the dire effects of Danny's murder, but it was a couple of months later that Emma encountered an incident which would cause her to realize just how much her life had changed—not just because of the murder, but stemming from the years of Mob intimidation and terror that had led up to the murder.

"I was sitting at the kitchen table struggling to write out Christmas cards, which was difficult in itself without having Danny around for the Holidays. I heard a noise by the back door and turned around to see the doorknob slowly turning back and forth. I grabbed my gun and immediately rushed the children out of the front door of the house and over to the neighbors' townhouse. By then, I was carrying a gun at all times for protection, just as Danny had taught me. I silently went back to the house by myself and looked around outside to see who it was. On some level, I probably hoped it was one of the men responsible for the death of my husband, so I could serve up some justice of my own. I would have done anything at that point to protect my family. However, it turned out to only be one of Joey's little friends who had been sent over by his parents at ten o'clock at night to borrow something from me. I was thinking at the time that I could have killed that child if I had let my fear take over and over-reacted."

At that moment, Emma had realized that things had forever changed for all of them, but things had especially changed for her. "I knew then that life was never going to be normal for me again," Emma remembers.

The beginning of 1975 would be an especially hard time for Emma. The full realization of her loss of economic support was upon her and the desperation of her financial future was revealing itself on a daily basis in the form of bills and the lack of cash to pay them. The weather that winter was particularly cold, and an intense blizzard that struck the Midwest in January seemed apropos of the dire position she found herself having to struggle through.

Emma now lived entirely for her children, and the pressures of being a single, unemployed mother were nothing compared to the ever-constant fear that she lived in: fear of the men from her past she knew were out there, fear for the safety of herself and her children, and fear of the uncertainty in her own future. She never rested. She was working sixteen hours per day, six days a week just in order to try and keep the business running, which was becoming a losing battle.

Emma tried desperately to make up for her lack of expertise, the know-how of her husband, but she knew it was only a matter of time before the company would have to close. For the next several months, she did everything she physically could to keep the business going, but it became just too much for her. Nine months after the murder, she realized she couldn't continue and the company wouldn't survive.

Emma first tried to sell the manufacturing plant, but no one would buy it, which forced her to have to sell off the equipment and then liquidate the inventory of products she had on the floor at that time. This at least gave her enough money to pay off the suppliers and then be able to take a few months off from work to spend time with her children and family; a chance to begin to recover on some level from her years of terror.

By November of 1975, she was able to find another job with her sister Judy at C.A. Roberts Company, a Chicago steel manufacturer, which was the same company Emma had worked at previously as a high school student. With this new job, she was able to at last provide for her children with a steady income and health insurance. It would also be the place where she would meet her next husband, someone she would years later describe as "the man who brought me back to earth."

In addition to landing the new job, a state relief agency, the Crime Victims Fund, provided the family with a $10,000 payment. "To us, this was a lot of money back in 1974," Emma recalls. "This really helped us to at least get back on our feet."

During that first year after Danny's murder, Emma had sacrificed everything for her kids. The efforts of that sacrifice took a terrible toll on her health. She suffered from chronic fatigue, which wasn't even recognized as an illness back in the 1970s. She endured repeated bouts of mononucleosis, which caused severe flu-like symptoms, including extreme fatigue that lasted for weeks. Ultimately, she was diagnosed with Lupus, a painful, potentially fatal disease that affects the entire body and causes painful joints, fevers, and unexplained skin rashes.

Not surprisingly, Emma's health issues and deep depression caused her to begin to turn to alcohol to try and deal with everything: the murder, the pain, the ceaseless struggle to survive mentally, emotionally, and physically, the illnesses, and the everyday fight to keep her family together. She was falling apart and simply surviving day-to-day at this point, trying to kill the pain chemically and using the desire to protect her children as her motive to stay alive.

Looking back on that time, Emma recalls, "I was drinking every day just to get through. I always had a gun on me and I began working with an FBI Agent to try to solve Danny's murder. He would come and pick me up after the children were in bed, and we would go to certain Mob hangouts. I thought at the time that I might see someone, recognize something, but I never did. We used to stop at a restaurant in Rosemont called Henrici's, on River Road. It was a very popular place back then and was a Mob hangout, and Danny and I even went there a few times. I don't really know what I was thinking that I could find. I was conflicted. I felt like I had to do something, but in reality, I was accomplishing nothing by this."

Emma spent several years working on and off with the agent, searching for clues and answers to who and why, looking for anything that she could use to convict the killers of her husband. But those efforts would prove futile and eventually faded away. Contact from the FBI diminished, until eventually she never heard from them anymore. During those earlier years while working with the FBI, Emma was never kept informed of anything related to the case. Neither she nor her family ever even received notification that the FBI was no longer actively investigating the murder. For almost thirty years, the Seiferts yearned for, but never received any answers from the police or the FBI about Danny's high-profile case.

Emma would come to find that after a few years, she would simply have to move on from clinging to the events of that terrible day and accept having to enter another phase of her life. While still wrought with apprehension, this would prove to be a much happier chapter for her. She would end up dating someone who was working with her at C.A. Roberts, and in 1982 the two would be married...temporarily closing, at least for a while, that destructive chapter in her life. But where Emma's quest had left off, Joe's and Nick's searches would begin.

As the two boys had grown older and had spent years watching the devastating effects the murder had on their mother, besides realizing how their own demons were brooding over the death of their father, they would begin looking for Danny's killers on their own. However, their searches would not employ help from the FBI or the police. They would instead walk in the footsteps of their father, uncles, and grandfather to search out the men responsible and then plan their own eye-for-an-eye retribution. But they would do this separately, unaware that the other was attempting the same.

Each would come to discover bits and pieces of vital information about the murder through their tireless and sometimes dangerous private investigations. They would also learn about their family's criminal past and more importantly, learn about the alleged mobsters to whom they were still connected through that bloodline.

The murderous events of that morning in 1974 were cataclysmic for the Seifert family. While the escape of the gunmen, at first, led some to think these men had gotten away with murder, there were two young Seifert boys who were about to grow into manhood and had vowed internally to leave no stone unturned in their search for the truth about the events of that day. Each of them was driven by thoughts of their mom and the experience of her suffering, and each decided that she deserved to be vindicated. As men, they would have no problem using their own connections to the underworld to seek answers. These answers would lead both to decide that justice would be administered to the men who had killed their father; even it was to be delivered by their own hands.

CHAPTER 11

Uncertainty

In the parallel world where mobsters rule, no one really knows for certain who can be trusted. This same distrust extends to police and even to Federal Investigators, as some have allegedly fallen under the influence of organized crime and others have even become associate members of the Mob.

Case in point would be that of Anthony "Twan" Doyle, a tough-looking Chicago cop who would be tried along with the other defendants in the Family Secrets Trial for his role in working directly for the Mob and passing information to imprisoned gangsters such as Mob leader, James "Little Jimmy" Marcello, who happened to also be on trial in the Family Secrets Trial.[34] Deciphering when a cop or Fed is probing a witness for information to solve a case, or rather to find out for the Mob exactly what that witness knows, can be a fine line; especially to people who find themselves in the periphery of Mob life.

As the investigation surrounding Danny's murder continued in the first two years after his death, Emma began to work tirelessly with several FBI agents who had been assigned to the case. She desperately wanted Danny's killers to be put away, and while she felt that the weight of the world was on her shoulders, just doing what she could to help solve her husband's murder might at least vindicate him on some level, as a victim.

During those years that she worked with the agents, questions about the Mob hit would begin to emerge concerning various pivotal circumstances that wouldn't get answered until many years later. These crucial, unanswered questions would turn out to provide valid evidence, and once again, they would hint at corruption and a cover-up. Except this time, the corruption wouldn't just point to corrupt business partners or mobsters.

One morning, some days after her return to running the company after Danny's murder, Emma was sitting at her desk when

---

[34] US Department of Justice, Operation Family Secrets
http://www.justice.gov/usao/iln/hot/familySecrets.html#Jul10

one of the FBI Agents who had appeared at Danny's wake walked in.

"He was one of the ones who had been assigned to me to investigate possible leads or connections," Emma recalls. "I thought when he showed up that they must have found something to help in the case. But once he came in, he said he was just stopping by to check up on me. He sat down across from me and we started to have a pretty general conversation. Right then, the phone rang and as I began to answer, a voice on the other line told me, 'I think you have something of ours.' I immediately recognized it to be Lombardo's voice. As flatly and coldly as I could, I told him that anything of theirs that I had was handed over to the FBI the day of Danny's murder."

Emma felt a cold chill come across her, as she heard the line disconnect. She thought it was strange that the call happened right as the Agent was sitting across from her. She dismissed the incident at that moment, but the timing set off red flags for her.

"I knew that Lombardo was looking to see what I might know, or what evidence Danny might have told me about. I knew he was searching for possible loose ends, which told me that I and my family were still in danger. The problem was that I was so distraught and terrified I really wasn't sure who I could trust. In this type of situation, any small thing could turn someone into a possible adversary or enemy. You just don't know."

In 1979, six Chicago-based FBI agents would later be assigned to Operation PENDORF[35], and the subsequent investigations behind the Mob's involvement with the Teamsters Union Central States Pension Fund. Decades later, one of these six agents, Pete Wacks, would discuss the Seifert murder and the resulting, temporary defeat for the Feds in an interview:

> Seifert possessed the necessary skills to run a successful business. He set up the molds and was the kind of straight man with the technical know-how that Mob figures cultivate when they infiltrate a legitimate business. But Lombardo was the silent partner. After Seifert was killed there just wasn't enough evidence to bring the case to the grand jury stage.[36]

Wacks would eventually be credited for being partly responsible for putting Lombardo, Dorfman, Williams, and two others away in December 1982 on charges of eleven counts of bribery, fraud, and conspiracy.[37] During his thirty-plus years of Mob investigative work for the FBI, Wacks got to know a lot of people

---

[35] O'Brien, John. "Retiring FBI Agent Recalls Bugging Hole in Teamsters Case." *Chicago Tribune*, March 31, 1997. http://articles.chicagotribune.com/1997-03-31/news/9703310046 1 wiretaps-pension-fund-teamsters-union

[36] "Illinois Police and Sheriff's News." *Organized Crime and Political Corruption*, 2006. http://www.ipsn.org/wacks.htm

[37] "Illinois Police and Sheriff's News." *Organized Crime and Political Corruption*. 2006. http://www.ipsn.org/wacks.htm

on both sides of the law quite well. To do his job, he had to know everyone.

Back then, the FBI didn't go undercover such as they do today; their agents worked and "developed"[38] associates to get them to flip and give the Bureau inside information. As a result, an agent might go to lunch one day with some straight-up cops or with a State's Attorney, and the next day might have drinks with well-known Mob associates in the constant effort to get them to work with the Feds. Lines were often crossed and/or blurred for an agent's end goal of convicting a known or suspected mobster. However, these blurred lines could lead down multiple ambiguous paths for an agent. Connections ran wide and deep, and sometimes it was just impossible to predict who knew or associated with whom, and more importantly, for what reasons.

At the time, what Emma didn't know was that law enforcement officials were also looking at Rosemont Illinois Mayor Donald E. Stephens, someone suspected but not fully proven, of having connections to the Chicago Outfit. In fact, Sam Giancana (back when he was in power) used to take Marshall Caifano's wife Darlene to an expensive motel called the Thunderbolt in Stephen's town of Rosemont, Illinois whenever her Mobster husband was out

---

[38] As described by Pete Wacks. "Illinois Police and Sheriff's News." *Organized Crime and Political Corruption*, 2006. http://www.ipsn.org/wacks.htm

of town on business. That motel, owned by Giancana, was well-known rendezvous point for the Mob and its mistresses, and was coincidentally later purchased by Donald Stephens.[39]

Stephens had taken control over the city of Rosemont as mayor in the 1950s, and kept that control through April of 2007, when he would end up losing a battle with stomach cancer. While never actually convicted of any crime, Donald Stephens had been indicted in two instances, but those charges were later dropped. The suspected Mob ties that he had, as well as those with clout whom he associated, would become apparent as evidenced in the late 1990s when he approached the state of Illinois with plans to build a casino in Rosemont.

The suspicion on part of the FBI extended through most of the time Stephens ran the city. In March of 2004, the village of Rosemont hired former FBI Agent Pete Wacks (then working as a private investigator [Wacks and Associates Ltd.]) to investigate Stephens' alleged ties to the Chicago Mob, "to determine whether Rosemont was connected to, associated with, or allowed operation of LCN-sponsored businesses or was connected to or associated with LCN members or associates."[40] Rosemont wanted the casino,

39 Tuohy, William, John. "The Rosemont Two Step." *American Mafia*,
    September 2002.
    http://www.americanmafia.com/Feature Articles 233.html
40 Affidavit. Peter J. Wacks. Investigation of Rosemont,
    Illinois, Donald A. Stephens, and ties to organized crime.
    http://www.ipsn.org/rosemont/wacks affidavit stephens.htm

and they figured who better to prove the innocence of its mayor than the former FBI agent who took down the very men to whom the Feds were linking Stephens.

Stephens was so sure the casino deal would go through, he began securing "donations" from interested parties and investors that included among many others, ex-con and Mob Associate Nick Boscarino, a former Teamsters official and former business partner of Stephens[41] when the two owned Eastern Services / American Trade Show Services; and William Daddano Jr., son of infamous Mobster hit-man William "Willie Potatoes" Daddano. Stephens also began to set up future construction contracts with companies such as D&P Construction, which had done waste-hauling work in Rosemont and whose co-owner was Josephine DiFronzo, sister-in-law of John "No Nose" DiFronzo, who today is considered the undisputed boss of the Chicago Mob. Stephens' direct involvement with the Mob may have been unproven, but his association with Mob members was quite clear.

An undercover FBI agent testified that on May 29, 1999 Mayor Donald Stephens met with five high-ranking Chicago

---

[41] Holt, Douglas and Michael Higgins. Rosemont Mayor Shifts Stand." *Chicago Tribune*, December 23, 2001. http://articles.chicagotribune.com/2001-12-23/news/0112230049_1_insurance-scheme-federal-grand-jury-ties

organized-crime figures, to discuss exactly what control the Mob would have over contracts at the casino.

Sitting with Stephens at Armand's restaurant in Elmwood Park were reputed Mob leader Joey 'The Clown' Lombardo, who is being sought by U.S. officials; John 'No Nose' DiFronzo; his brother Peter; Joe 'The Builder' Andriacchi; and Rudy Fratto, among others," said John Mallul, head of the FBI's organized crime unit in Chicago.[42]

This alleged meeting was fiercely disputed by Stephens, and he continued with plans for the casino. Stephens went so far as to begin having the site prepped for construction and hired DiFronzo's company, D&P Construction to haul the waste. But in 2001 after a thorough investigation, the state's Gaming Board announced a reversal of their original issuance of a gaming license to Emerald Casino and Rosemont. This decision, remarkably, was red-flagged by a small $400 political donation[43] that was discovered by the Board, which was given to Stephens from D&P Construction.

The 2001 statement read as follows:

---

[42] Chase, John. "FBI Links Emerald Casino, Mob, and Mayor of Rosemont, Illinois." Chicago Tribune, July 19, 2005. http://articles.chicagotribune.com/2005-07-19/news/0507190223_1_illinois-gaming-board-rosemont-mob

[43] Rosemont Mayor Returns Mob-Linked Funds." *Better Government Association*, 2008. http://www.bettergov.org/rosemont_mayor_returns_mob-linked_funds/

The owner of D&P, Josephine DiFronzo, is married to Peter DiFronzo and is the sister-in law of John DiFronzo, individuals who have been identified as known members of organized crime. Emerald's failure to exercise appropriate supervision resulted in work being performed at the site by D&P.[44]

As a result, the Board yanked the license from Emerald and Rosemont. Stephens and his investors were temporarily out of luck.

While ultimately determined by Pete Wacks that "The Mayor is or was neither connected to or associated with any of the [...] individuals [Sam Giancana, William Messina, John DiFronzo, Peter DiFronzo, Anthony Daddino, Joseph Andriacchi, Joseph Lombardo, Jack Cerone]"[45], guilt by association can shed a powerful light upon the murky Chicago underworld that the Mob controls. It is this association that decades later, would send a chill down Emma's spine looking back on those first years after her husband's murder.

"I was reading a book about a corrupt FBI agent who was 'playing' an individual he was supposed to be protecting, for information," she recalls.

---

[44] Fusco, Chris. "Gaming Board bans Trash Firm over Family Ties / The Mob in Plainfield." The Plainfield Forum, December 23, 2002. http://www.topix.com/forum/city/plainfield-il/TKE1CU16HIL59BPSB

[45] Affidavit. Peter J. Wacks. Investigation of Rosemont, Illinois, Donald A. Stephens, and ties to organized crime. http://www.ipsn.org/rosemont/wacks_affidavit_stephens.htm

"I set the book down, and I remembered the phone call from Lombardo in the office that day and I thought it was so strange, the timing of Lombardo calling just after the agent had walked in."

Emma remembers, "Now that I look back, you just can't ignore the timing of the agent showing up unexpectedly at the one and only exact time Lombardo would call the company and ask about something of theirs that I supposedly had."

She continues, "I remember noticing that the agent observed me very closely when I was on the phone with Lombardo too, which at the time I took simply as the close eye of an on-duty FBI agent. This and the years off and on of agents coming by at strange times of the night, taking me out to Mob hangouts to supposedly look for clues, which we never found anything. I just get a very bad feeling from it all. Like I was involved possibly not for my protection necessarily, but in reality to make sure that I wasn't hiding something. It's a terrible thought. But when you go through an experience such as this, you come to realize that anyone around you could be connected. Even the man next to you who says he's there to help. In the end, you just never know."

Nick states, "It's a puzzle that you have to continually put together. And each piece is connected to another, and another, and another. There are politicians who were very powerful and had a lot of influence, and had ties not only to the Outfit leaders, but also to the Teamsters and to casinos whether here [Chicago] or in Vegas.

And now, just because this isn't 1974 anymore doesn't mean there isn't money, a lot of money, to be made by the Outfit from gambling. And whatever city gets a casino, you can bet there are millions floating out to the politicians that made it happen, even though you'll never prove it. Why do you think they always push so hard for it?"

Emma admits there is no real evidence to show any definitive corrupt link with the agents who were working with her, but she cannot help but see the years of wasted meetings, surveillance, and the repeated, probing questions about the same subject. She remembers one agent constantly asking, "Are you sure you don't know anything that these guys would be interested in you for? Are you sure Danny didn't leave something for you just in case?"

"Back then, I just took it as the FBI looking for answers," Emma recalls. "And maybe they genuinely were. But as the years went by and I saw no action being taken, I started to question it all. That is something I'll never be able to prove, and I'll never know the real purpose for that questioning."

The Seifert's perspective comes not only from speculation, but is based on decades of experience and basic street-smarts. Danny's partners knew and paid local police to keep things quiet. Danny himself knew that they'd get away with burning down International Fiberglass because of the corrupt individuals they knew working for the city. They knew the investigation would be dismissed by the higher-ups.

187

Joe points out, "These guys [the police and Federal Investigators] have a very dangerous and tough job and they have to continually play one person off of another just to get a step ahead. In the end, you just can never know what their true intention is. You wanna believe it's genuine; the help they are providing you."

"But with the example of the agents working with my mom," Joe continues, "they may have been using mom to dig for information for the later case against Lombardo rather than dad's murder. They may have been digging to make sure she didn't know anything that Lombardo might have an interest in, for their own investigation's purposes, or maybe to feed it to Lombardo to gain his trust so that the agents could get closer to him. These are the types of connections that are so embedded you'll never dig through them. The players of these games will always have a second agenda, whether it is for the good guys or the bad guys, or both."

Nick adds, "You certainly can't ignore that the FBI is credited with putting Lombardo away years later. But with everything she's been through and what our family knows, trust comes only to very few people near to us and suspicion gets thrown on many. My question is, if they could convict Lombardo now with the same evidence they had in 1974, why couldn't the FBI take care of Lombardo back then? Why did it take 30 years?"

The Seiferts found that they needed the law's help to find answers to convict those who were involved with the 1974 murder.

Yet even more, they also needed the help of criminals to find the truth out for themselves. Through years of probing, both Joe and Nick realized that not only could they not fully trust the intentions of the law, but that ironically, it would take associates of the very people that killed Danny to lead them to the real answers to the questions that surround the murder.

The Seiferts' suspicions and doubts will never be resolved and will always be unanswered, but those grounded suspicions point to the very core of the problem—that the legal and criminal worlds are often entangled. A symbolic representation of this entanglement can be found in prison, where inmates often get web tattoos on their elbows to mark that they've done time. The web signifies the inescapable trap they have found themselves in. Yet it also signifies the ever-present entanglement and connecting lines that make up the virtual web that exists between the law and the criminals that exist outside of the law. It is a web that snares and traps individuals and prevents escape, just as in the situation that Danny had found himself. It is often others, the forgotten victims of murder and crime, who find themselves trapped in that same web not for just a sentence of time, but for life. Danny's family, as they fought for normalcy, answers, and survival, realized they will most likely, never find a way out.

CHAPTER 12

Frantic Lines

The four-year-old boy who witnessed the men storm into his parents' company and ultimately kill his father would be forever changed by those events. The innocent times he had known in his short life, times that most kids get to enjoy for many years, came to a brutal and abrupt end.

Before that day, Emma remembers, "Joey was no different than any other of his friends in the neighborhood. He was always laughing. He and Danny had a very close relationship and the two would play together all the time. Even when the pressure was at the worst for Danny, Joey could always put a smile on his face."

Flash forward to present-day, and Joe Seifert is a tough, unafraid father of two with an uncanny resemblance to his murdered father. Those who know his darker side call him "Joker." While this nickname came about for reasons unrelated to his past, it ultimately stuck as a dark reference to his unofficial godfather, the "Clown."

Such resemblances would not go unnoticed during the Family Secrets Trial as proven during the jury selection process, when Joey Lombardo objected to a potential juror who looked a lot like Danny Seifert. Lombardo rose out of his chair and yelled out to the courtroom, "That's him! That's him! That's a ghost from my past!" Following that lead, Joe played up his likeness to Danny and grew his hair for the trial to match how his dad had worn his hair at the time of the murder. Joe would sit in the courtroom and stare at Lombardo, intent on conjuring up any "ghosts" he could to haunt the man sitting opposite of him, whom he knew killed his father.

Joe has full-sleeve tattoo work on both of his arms, serving as self-inflicted physical scars that hint to the inescapable memories of his father's murder—and Joe's subsequent quest for revenge years later. His left arm features a sadistic clown hovering over an image of a doll with its eyes sewn shut, and a clock frozen in the time of his father's death—8:25am; a dark homage to his father and a permanent reminder of the man, his own namesake, Joey "the Clown" Lombardo, whom Joe feels destroyed his family and his future.

On a daily basis, Joe walks an intricate line of father and guardian of his own family, while he still feels the blood of a Mob lineage pulse through his veins. He constantly looks over his shoulder. In part this is to look for people that may want to do him or his family harm, friends or associates of Lombardo perhaps, but mostly out of pure instinct for survival.

"I wanted Joey Lombardo dead," Joe freely states as he reflects on his decision years ago to go and find the men responsible for his father's death.

"Of course I did. To be honest, I had the tools to do it. To me, it was always only Lombardo. I knew there were others involved, but it was Lombardo that pulled the strings that made it happen. He was the closest to my father at the time. I knew that he was told to "manage" my father, and when the order came down after they had become uncomfortable with how things were going, it's only protocol that he [Lombardo] would have had the personal connection to it."

When Joe reflects on the Mob's decision to kill his father, he takes the same cold attitude as they did; "It was business," he says in a matter-of-fact tone as he reflects on that day. "I know that. They didn't care about him or certainly our family; or the future of our family. Hell, Lombardo would have killed his own mother if the Mob told him to do so. They were concerned about protecting what was close to them, which was the money. Well, after I grew up I took the same approach. One way or another, I decided that Lombardo would have to pay. It was just business for me too, but it's my family's business; or rather, my business to protect my family."

After Joe decided that Lombardo would have to pay for his crime "one way or another," it would be many years before he and his family would be contacted by the FBI and told that their case was being included in the Family Secrets Trial. Back then, he felt there was no way the FBI was ever going to prosecute anyone for the murder. "The only other possible way," he concluded, "was through my own connections."

There are a lot of people in this world who will brag of knowing "bad" people; those people that can take care of things for a price. With Joe Seifert, these are far from bragging rights. They are simply a fact of his life. His contacts are far from mere name-dropping images; he knows how to interact with them and is known and respected by them. Taking after the lineage of his father and uncles, Joe is someone who has known a lot of people on both sides of the law for most of his life.

This heritage becomes evident even at the simplest of his life's moments. When Joe meets someone for lunch or dinner, he is on alert. He sits with his back to the wall and unconsciously studies everyone in the room. At any given moment, he can discuss what cars have pulled in and exited a parking lot that is visible through the windows. Some may call this "paranoia," but to both Joe and his brother Nick, this is how they were raised. It is purely innate to them. There is no thought process to it—they are always on guard.

Joe recalls when he and his ex-wife were getting married, he told her, "You were raised in the *Brady Bunch*; I was raised in *Goodfellas*.[46]" For Joe and Nick, even though Emma did her best to shield them as children, their observations of her constant state of peril, of being on edge for their first few years, was absorbed entirely into their outlook on society.

"Besides the clear image of my father's blood splattering on the wall, I really have few memories of my childhood before the age of eight or so, other than a couple instances of my mother screaming out a window, or one time flipping the dinner table over in a fit of rage," Joe recalls. "She went through a lot, and I do remember her being sick all the time. It was hard for her to do much of anything. But looking back, she was working so hard and had so much stress, who could blame her? She still managed to raise us, and give us the best she could, which was a whole hell of a lot."

When Emma eventually remarried in 1982, she moved the family to Yorba Linda, California, just inland from the sun-baked beaches of Southern California. Joe would enter his teenage years a

---

[46] IMDB http://www.imdb.com/title/tt0099685/

world away from the Mob, Chicago, and everything he had known growing up.

"I loved California," Joe says, reminiscing about his years in seventh and eighth grades. "I spent a lot of time in Huntington Beach and I loved the ocean. I really had a lot of fun out there. But after only a couple years, my parents needed to move back to Chicago for work. So, despite my objections, we went back. It wasn't long before I started going through some typical teenage stuff, getting in fights, etc. Mom always used to try to keep me on track, but I think it was probably inevitable that I'd start down a darker path; same with Nick."

Even though Emma did her best to give them a normal life, she knew that as Joe and Nick grew up, they were bound to have some questions that would be related to their father's murder. When these questions did surface, they would initially be brushed off by various family members, thereby only increasing her sons' curiosities.

"I never really wanted to ask mom, as she was so sick all the time and I didn't want to upset her," Joe recalls. "So I would go to the library and look up newspaper articles related to the murder. Years later I even went to the Bensenville Police and asked them questions, but all I ever heard was, 'Sorry we can't comment on an active case.' I thought to myself, 'Bullshit active, it's been how many years? Who's still working on it?'"

"I didn't find out till much later that mom actually had all the newspaper clippings on every article there was on his murder," Joe continues, "as well as the events leading up to it! I was pissed at first, because a lot of the answers were right there under our noses. The newspapers spelled it out; even people in my family knew who were involved. But whenever I would ask, no one in my family really wanted to tell me so as not to upset me. I don't know, maybe they were just hoping I'd let it rest, but they should have known better."

For Joe, the real question then became not just who was the trigger-man (or men), but who was *directly* responsible. Who was it that ran the hit?

"There is a small difference on the surface," he states, "but a huge difference underneath. The person responsible, who coordinated it or even authorized it, might as well be the same person who pulled the trigger in my eyes. With them, the connection is much closer. Any professional hit-man can walk up to a stranger and put a bullet in their head for the right price, and still be able to sleep at night. You have to look for the person who is responsible for it. That is the person who is closely tied to that victim. A murder is usually personal."

It wasn't until a few years after high school that Joe began to mix with some people who could give him more than just a newspaper article.

"I was working as a warehouse manager for quite a few years," Joe recalls. "In that job, you start to know the drivers that come in and out, some of the warehouse guys, the construction guys, you know. Well, a lot of them were connected to various motorcycle clubs and Mob people around Chicago. Everybody knows somebody in this town, whether they realize it or not. I happened to get in with a couple of guys in particular and we started to go hang out on weekends. Not a real big deal. There was always a party around for us to hit, and that's really what it was all about."

At first, Joe was just hanging around them once in a while, and he didn't even have his own motorcycle to begin with.

"I realized that I needed to get a bike in order to hang with these guys for real, and one day I was looking at bikes during lunch at the local shop, and there she sat; as sweet as could be," Joe recalls. "A tricked-out Harley Davidson with a flame paint-job and all."

"The guy told me five grand and I immediately called a friend and borrowed the money. The next day I called my wife and told her I'd be late because I just bought a Harley. She didn't believe me but sure enough, there I am screaming down the 294 Toll-way on the way home that night, never even ridden before on the street," Joe remembers, laughing. "I pulled up to our driveway on the bike and she couldn't believe it! She didn't know whether to laugh, cry, or be pissed off!"

Joe also began to meet some other people who had more connections. He would always make it a point to see how far in he could get with someone, just to see who or what they knew. And some of these contacts ended up becoming really good friends of his.

"It was sort of like putting a big puzzle together," Joe remembers. "I was having fun with it. I knew the end result that I wanted, which was to get to Lombardo. I just needed to see how to do it; and in order to get to someone like that, a Mob heavy, you need to have some serious inside info. And that information doesn't come easily or quickly. I'd happen to run into someone connected through a friend, and I'd throw out a question here and there, 'Do you know this guy or that guy, how would I get to so-and-so,' you know, always probing."

Some contacts helped, some didn't. Yet Joe began to gradually build his connections, and he made progress. But this progress came with a price. People in the "circle" don't just throw out information to anyone. Trust has to be earned and Joe had a lot of time to earn it, but it would cost him more than he could realize at the time.

As he got closer to his biker friends, he realized some walked a far more dangerous line than others. "These guys were independent of the typical motorcycle club. They were sort of like free agents, and prided themselves on flying solo," he remembers.

"And those are the guys that I became very good friends with. While they may have had links to this club or that club, they ran by no one else's rules, which to me, was something that really hit home."

Joe decided to blur the line even more and start to work with certain people to do favors. "Sure, part of it was to build trust, but another part was that I liked these guys, and for once I really felt like I fit in," he remembers.

"I'd help to coordinate meetings with some guys to meet others that wanted to get together for reasons that I didn't need or necessarily want to know. Between that and even organizing some other meetings myself, I became entrenched with those guys. They knew I was real; they knew I could hang and they began to trust me and rely on me. If we were out and one of them got in a fight, I'd jump in no questions asked. That built my cred with them, as well as with all of the other contacts I made."

At the time, Joe's wife had no idea any of this was going on. "I'd just tell her that I was going for a ride on a Saturday with the guys, and that's it," he recalls. "I'd call her a couple hours later and tell her we made it, and I'd be home that night. I was spending a lot of time with all of these guys, and I was getting to know them really well and vice versa. It's a great feeling to know that no matter what, someone's got your back. That's a feeling that I never really had before, at least not from someone other than a family member. To this day, there are only a couple of people in my life that I fully trust."

199

The deeper Joe got in with his contacts, the more he was sure that they would be able to help him go after Lombardo.

"I began to see and hear of things that most people would want to run from," Joe recalls. I knew guys who talked freely about the various crimes they committed, how they made big money here or there. I went to a place once in a while that's now torn down, where they did some of their 'business.' They called it 'The Warehouse' and it was an old, closed-down warehouse in the Chicago area. They told me, 'Anything that goes in doesn't come out—ever.' When you walked in, it was straight out of a horror movie. It was dark, the ground was all wet, water dripping from pipes, chains hanging from the ceilings—every ounce of you lit up inside and you knew it was a bad place to be. It was all you could do to muster the strength to stay inside."

Joe continued to hone his skills and made even more contacts. Besides his darker contacts, he had also become friends with some ex-cops working as private investigators that would look up information for him. He laughs as he recalls, "They told me that they'd look up this or that for me, as long as I could promise they weren't going to read about it in the paper the next day!"

Through his contacts, both good and bad, he learned things no normal middle-class person would ever dream of, such as what rivers around the city had the fast currents and deep silt beds, which would ensure anything thrown in, such as evidence, would not be found. This was important to him, as he felt that it put him closer to the mindset of the men who killed his father.

"I really was living two lives at once," he remembers of this time in his life. "I'd be the first to admit that I wasn't a nice person back then. I saw a lot of bad things and it had become unclear where one part of me ended and the other began. That line had blurred. One minute I was living as 'Joker' and doing this or that, making connections, making money, riding, having a great fucking time. Then after a 45-minute ride, I'm back to 'North Shore Joe' again. I'd come home to a nice suburban house with a fenced-in yard, a wife, and two kids and a dog. This home would be anyone's dream-come-true; anyone's but mine at the time."

Joe's past and his blocked-out memories were beginning to catch up to him. He began to lose himself, and it was happening faster and faster. He lost the social-identity control that should have grounded him to his family.

"Fear is intoxicating. It's powerful to know that you could do what you wanted whenever you wanted to do it," Joe says matter-of-factly. "Knowing those types of people is definitely scary. I've seen some pretty crazy shit and some things that just make your stomach turn. I knew very well that I was crossing a line of no-return, but I also knew that this is exactly where I needed to be to find the answers that I wanted to find. I was torn between who I *wanted* to be—the father I didn't have—and who I *liked* to be.

201

Honestly, I was having fun and feeling at home more with the people that I had met then I ever did anywhere else in my life. I wasn't sure if I could ever really go back to being just Joe. I'm still not sure."

While his search for Lombardo was never "a day-to-day thing," it was always in the back of his mind. Joe would do some business with his biker contacts and if he ran into someone he thought could help, he'd try to get more information. Mainly he was just having fun being himself, something that he really hadn't experienced before.

"I basically just wanted to find a time that I knew he [Lombardo] would be somewhere," Joe remembers. "At first, I wanted to just find him; to look him straight in the eye. I knew what I *wanted* to do to him, but I didn't know what I *would* do. Part of me felt that if I ran into him, it didn't matter if it was on the street, in a grocery store, or at the theater, I'd have a chance to do really anything I wanted. If I wanted to kill him, I could. But that type of information, the exact time and place someone high-up in the organization like him will be somewhere is never accurate. Shit, he lived half the time at friends' houses so his activities and locations were never the same. He was very hard to nail down."

After years of hanging out with people and gaining the trust of who he had met, Joe had a breakthrough that would lead him to what he had been searching for.

"One of the guys knew some people out in Vegas," Joe remembers. "It turned out that Lombardo would go out there for some business at a strip bar once in a while, and they got wind that he would be out there because someone was having trouble at a certain club. It just so happened that back then I was thinking of starting up an electronics business and there was an electronics convention going on out there right at the same time."

Joe realized that he could easily arrange to be out there the same days that Lombardo would be, through the guise of being at the convention for his business. The question would be how to pull off the trick of running into him. Here, is when his years of developing his close friendships would come into play.

"One of the main guys in the club approached me and told me that he heard about how I was trying to find Lombardo," Joe recalls. "It turned out that he told me he could pull some strings to help make it happen. He knew who Lombardo was and who he was connected to, but this guy didn't care. His question to me was simple; 'When do you want it to happen, and do you want to be there?'"

At that point, Joe wanted to put it in motion. He knew that he had options; but this was no longer just about finding Lombardo. He had the opportunity to take him out, and he knew it was for real, and most likely that it wouldn't fail. Almost without thinking, he began to make plans to head out to Vegas.

"It wasn't so much if I could control these guys and run the plan," he recalls, "it was more about controlling myself. I knew that finding him, finding out proof-positive that he did it, that he controlled the hit against my father, wouldn't be enough for me. I knew what I was capable of and once I had him in front of me; there was no way I could stop."

Joe started to put together a list of people he could trust as alibis, in case something went wrong and might bounce back to him. He, like his father, had kept everything about his quest from his wife to protect her and his family. He knew full well that this was a decision whose impact he would have to carry with him the rest of his life. It would be something that could potentially tear him or even his family apart, yet could also bring him a peace of mind that he had never experienced.

As the time to meet up with Lombardo came closer, Joe felt strangely calm—totally at peace. He knew in his heart that he could do it, if he really wanted to. He knew that deep down, whatever the cost, he wanted to put a bullet in Lombardo's head. Yet what hindered him despite all the years he had spent looking for Lombardo and networking with gangsters, was the potential for violent repercussions that could reach his family.

"I knew that if I took him out, there was a chance, no matter how small, that it would come back to me," he recalls. "It bothered me. This wasn't some low-level shit. I was thinking of killing someone; and not just anyone, a Mob heavy. If I were caught, I could go to jail or worse, they could come after my wife or kids. I could be setting in motion for my kids exactly what was set in motion for me thirty-plus years ago."

Joe unexpectedly found himself in a similar position that his father was in. Should he do what he wanted to do, or do what he felt was best for his family? The decision came easily.

"Just one day before I was supposed to leave, I called it all off," he states. "Every day I tell myself it was the right thing to do, especially when I am with my family or when I see my kids at school events. But every day, I also think about what I could have done for my father, my mother, and myself—that I could have been the one to serve Lombardo a fate he truly deserved. In some ways, I do regret it—not making that meeting in Vegas, not running into my father's murderer. But I made the decision to be there for my kids, which is something my father didn't get the chance to do. So in that, I know he would have been proud of my decision. I feel that he would have told me to do the same."

Not long after Joe's change of heart, Emma continued to try and insulate her children from the effects of that day and was yet unaware of just how close Joe had come to exacting his revenge. On the 25th anniversary of Danny's murder, she asked Joe to meet her at Danny's grave to have a private ceremony.

"I told Joe that we needed to bury the past," Emma recalls. "It was clear to me that this was affecting him still; I could sense it in him. At the time, I felt there would never be justice in the case. For Joe's well-being and the well-being of his family, I asked him to meet me there on the anniversary of his father's murder."

For this ceremony, Joe took a book with him that was in print titled, *The Enforcer* by William Roemer. This book is about Mob hit-man Anthony Spilotro and within, had many references to his father and his father's murder. For the Seiferts, the book somehow validated their experience and became something personally symbolic of the past twenty-five years, and of the constant struggle for survival over those decades.

"We put the book in a plastic bag, dug a small hole, and buried it near his tombstone," Joe remembers. "With that, we attempted to say goodbye, and try to move on. But deep down, I think we both knew that would never really happen."

For the Seifert family, moving on would never be easy. Only a few years later, in 2003, Emma would get a phone call from the FBI that would shake the very foundation of her family and would once again start in her a process of reliving those terrifying moments all over. While at first, Joe thought the trial would finally be a positive step toward finally getting all of the answers for which he had searched, he and his family slowly began to realize it would only recall and reinforce their decades of pain, and cause some of the family to slip even deeper into torment. The intricate and dangerous line that Joe tenuously walked throughout his adult life would no longer be blurred—he would come to find it destroyed.

CHAPTER 13

Road Trip

Danny's murder had put Nick into an especially difficult situation. As the oldest son, he not only took on the responsibility of helping to care for Joe and Kathy, but also had to watch helplessly as Emma battled depression, and then saw her health deteriorate. Most of Nick's childhood friends had disappeared, either too afraid themselves of his family's connections or forbidden by their own parents to be around him. The details of his father's murder and Mob connections had made the newspaper headlines as well as being a focus of the local TV media coverage.

"I was embarrassed by it, to be honest," Nick recalls. "I guess you can't really blame my friends or their parents back then, but none of them knew what I was going through or what it did to me to lose my friends so quickly after losing my father. It was tormenting."

As Nick grew older, he grew tired of always having to hide what happened to his father or who his family had been connected to. He became more withdrawn and focused on just living day-to-day; a trait born of family tragedy but honed into a keen survival tool that he would carry and come to rely on throughout his life.

His teenage years were a particularly difficult time for Nick, who grew up a troubled young man. Besides bouncing back and forth between living with Emma and his birth mother, Nick had tried to quit school several times. Emma would have none of it. She remembers, "I just did my best to keep him on track to finish school, which was quite difficult at times. I had to at least get him to that finished point and then he would enter manhood with as much as I could possibly have given him on my own."

When Nick did finish high school, college wasn't an option for him. He was eighteen years old and needed a job and money. Down the street from their house in Bensenville, Illinois was Gun World, a large shooting range and gun shop that he used to pass by all the time he was in school. After responding to an advertisement that Gun World had put in their window for help behind the counter, he was hired and started down a path that would lead him to a career. Naturally drawn to guns from his father's influence and being raised around them, it was a good fit for him.

After starting the job, he did well and quickly took on a number of different jobs within the shop, including reloading cartridges, running the pistol range, working behind the sales counter, and managing the range logs. His experience reloading the cartridges taught him how to adjust the loads for different uses, such as using just enough gunpowder to deliver a round to a certain distance but still keep the report relatively quiet. Working at the shop also required him to be authorized to carry a handgun and he learned how to shoot very well. He practiced with many different types of handguns and learned the nuances of their operations and how to handle the different calibers for firing accurately. The interest his father had sparked years ago in weapons was now being honed to a fine level.

Through his later teen years, Nick had repeatedly talked to his uncles about his father. He was always trying to probe them for information on the murder. He, like Joe, knew there was much more to the story; sinister things that no one was telling him, and he knew that his uncles were keeping information from the family to avoid further Mob intimidation.

Finally, responding to the relentless young man's questions, Nick's uncles began to give him very discreet hints and clues to the background and circumstances of that day and the people who were linked to it.

"Sometimes it would be a name I'd never heard of, a street, or something like that," Nick recalls. "It would then be up to me to go hunting."

Nick had also made some friends with some ex-cops who would occasionally help him trace a name or number down. His work at the range also gave him access to run checks on people of interest and track down people's hangouts or addresses. His thirst for answers to his father's murder began to grow into an obsession, and his job became a perfect vehicle for the searching that he needed to do on his own.

One day when Nick was in the back of the gun shop managing the range, a man came in and asked for him specifically. He approached Nick but didn't introduce himself. He simply told him that he knew something about his father's murder. If there was any part of Nick that was not yet consumed with the need to find answers, it was lost at that moment.

"I had never been approached by someone like that," Nick recalls of the incident. "I was probably nineteen years old or so, and was still inexperienced at how to interact with connected guys like that. All of a sudden I had someone telling me information on my father's murder; telling me that he was sorry it happened, etc. I stood there listening to the guy and while I wasn't afraid, especially because

I was armed, it was a moment that changed my life because at that second I knew there was a truth to all of this, somewhere."

The man gave Nick details and said that it was all about money related to the Teamsters, and then asked Nick if he knew who was involved.

"I told him that I thought it was Lombardo and Frank Cullotta, but he never responded to the names. The conversation ended and that was that. He may have been probing to see what I knew, or maybe to see what my family knew. You never know with those guys. Something like this never goes away, and they might have been trying to see if we were letting it lie, or if we were looking for information and maybe more."

About a year later, Nick would get a chance to learn who the mysterious informant was.

"I was working the sales counter, and one morning the same guy walked in and went back to the range to practice. He never saw me. Customers who went to the range had to sign in and show their state IDs or drivers licenses, so I knew that I could get his name and track him down. I went to the book, took his name down and had a friend check it out. I'd never heard of the guy, but after doing some checking, it turned out he was a lower level Outfit guy, probably someone that knew enough of the facts to either take a personal interest, since the murder was well recognized as a big fuck-up by the Mob leadership. Or he may have been sent by someone higher up to see what I knew or what I thought; or maybe even if I was out looking for people."

Nick never spoke to the stranger again, but he began to dig deeper for other information. His uncles were still passing on hints here and there to him, but had to be especially discreet because of their own connections and for fear of reprisals.

"Absolutely nothing could get back to them," Nick says. "I had to make sure that no matter what, my investigations didn't rattle the wrong cages and put my uncles in the crosshairs of someone's interest."

"My uncle Tom had come to live with us for a couple months in 1973," Nick remembers. "Tom was well-connected on the same level as my father had been. He knew these people too and also what they were capable of. Right before I had started working at the range, I spoke to him and he told me that he tried to get my father to not testify, but he wouldn't listen to him. Shortly after that conversation with me, Tom took off to the west coast and I lost track of him for many years. I became closer to Bob however, and he would continue to feed me facts and leads to track down."

Nick became an expert at cross-referencing names or any other information he could get his hands on. He'd dig through phone books for names and track down their addresses. He'd profile them, their families, their habits, and follow them to learn their daily patterns. Nick would bounce information back to his uncle about other people he had come to know, and would get a "hot or cold" response so that he could adjust his efforts. Once Nick was satisfied that the individual he was researching had viable information or was someone tied to other people who might know something, he planned to approach them.

"I always took my time," Nick recalls as he describes his methods. "I was patient. I waited until they were vulnerable and made absolutely sure that they were alone so that I wouldn't get jumped or possibly lured into a trap if they suspected they were being followed."

Nick remembers one individual in particular whom he learned had some information.

"I approached him in the middle of a grocery store on Grand Avenue," Nick recalls. "You gotta remember there weren't cameras all over back then like there are now. I walked up to him and let him know right away that I was armed and convinced him that I was ready to take him out then and there because of what he knew. He was alone and became scared once he realized exactly who I was. People who read this need to understand that at the time, I had nothing to lose, and this guy knew it too. But he wanted to walk away and go home to his family. That is what gave me my power when I approached someone. They knew that I had nothing to lose, and that I wouldn't hesitate. It was personal, which is what ended up opening many doors for me."

What happened next gave Nick what he considers his big breakthrough, and what would launch him on an ever-increasing, more fruitful search for the definitive proof of who was responsible for his father's death.

"The guy looked at me and told me he didn't have anything to do with it, but that he knew who did and would give me the names. He spilled the names right there in the cereal aisle as I pressed my gun into him. He told me it was Tony Spilotro, John Fecarotta, Joe Hansen, Frank Schweihs, Angelo LaPietra, Joey Lombardo, and Jackie Cerone."

Nick was stunned. Everyone suspected Lombardo from the start, but why had all the rest of these guys been there? He had never heard of Joe Hansen, who turned out to be a drifter hit man for the Mob. Hansen never carried an ID, only used cash, and lived in some of Schweihs' apartment buildings so that he couldn't be traced. And if Cerone, a senior Outfit member, was involved, it meant that Danny's murder was definitely a top-priority hit for the Outfit, and a problem that they took very serious.

Almost unconsciously, Nick was driven to take revenge. His efforts began as someone looking for answers, but as his methods intensified, he became someone who was out for vengeance.

"I never thought about it," Nick states. "It just became what I did. I knew that one day I wanted to take out the man who killed my father, and I wouldn't stop until I had the information."

Nick decided that to go after these guys would take a top-down approach.

"If you hit a lower guy then everyone above him would know something's coming and take action to avoid it," Nick describes. "I knew that people were getting feedback that I was searching for something. I had to plan this correctly to truly find who was responsible. I would have to continue to be patient, even though all roads pointed to Lombardo."

Nick's investigations began to take on a new level after moving to Florida when he was in his early twenties. There were plenty of mobsters living in the Sunshine State, and by this time Nick knew exactly where to find them. The ones outside of Chicago also felt less hesitant to give him information, since they were away from their local territory, and Nick was able to find out information not only about his father's murder, but others as well.

"These guys began to understand that I wasn't searching on behalf of the cops or the Feds or anything like that," Nick describes. "They realized that this was my own hunt, and many began to respect that. They all felt that what happened to my father was fucked up and I began to gain their confidence. They knew that I was no different than they were, and that this was a family thing; completely outside the law."

Nick found out early on that at times, he really knew more than the Feds because of his inside connections.

"One of my contacts told me about the Dorfman murder," Nick recalls. "I was told that the murder wasn't done by Spilotro like it was stated in the papers. I also was told it was done by two individuals, with two different caliber of pistols, which the papers only discussed one."

"I was told that Schweihs was there and shot him twice with his .22 when the gun jammed," Nick continues. "It was then that Fecarotta took over with his gun and shot him four more times with an unusual round, a .32. This was kept from the papers by the Feds because they didn't want anyone to suspect that they knew it was two shooters. They just had no idea who the shooters were. I finally heard the correct answer years later but I have no idea how the Feds found out."

Nick's source was someone he'd known for years.

"We'd meet in parking lots, go for lunch, whatever," Nick remembers. "Once the Family Secrets trial started, the judge wanted me to give up my sources because I kept coming up with information on certain people's whereabouts before the Feds could do it on their own. I was called before the Grand Jury twice in 2004 and I stood there in front of everyone and said, 'Fuck if I'll tell you anything, you can throw me in jail for contempt.' The FBI agent that was working with us at the time smoothed things over, but that judge was out for me to give shit up. These people were the only ones giving me any bit of truth, why the hell would I give any of them up? Who the hell did the judge think he was talking to?"

Nick remembers, "I got more and more pissed about it, and began thinking they [the Feds] would just fuck this whole thing up again. It got to the point where every time I'd come into town, I'd have to check in with the FBI and sign documents stating I wouldn't do this or that. Of course I couldn't tell mom or Joe what it was all about, but they started wondering why I always had to sign something and why the Feds would fly me in and then right back out the next day!"

Nick's investigations in Florida led him to become certain that he was closing in on the very people that the Feds were closing in on, albeit for different, more efficient purposes. And through his investigations, Nick always wrestled with the problem of Lombardo.

"Everything pointed to him," Nick reflects on his search. "But I never saw dad mad at Joey. I never saw them fight or argue. It was always "Uncle Joey" until the murder and then I never saw him again. Deep down, even with what everything people were telling me, even the people on the inside, it wasn't so much that I didn't believe it, it was that I didn't *want* to believe it. I was really conflicted. I knew the reason that I was looking for him was for retribution. I needed it to be a sure thing in my own mind, not just an assumption or based only off of what others had told me."

"But what did it for me was when I was told how it went down," Nick recalls. "I learned that Spilotro was the one who took dad's gun away. Schweihs was the one who was supposed to handcuff him but fucked it up, allowing dad to be able to fight them off and leave the building. I found out that their intention was not just to kill him. They were going to take him away and torture him. That's why there were so many men there that morning. They could have easily just had a sharp shooter in the parking lot hit him when he stepped out of the car, but that's not what they did. They had nine guys there that day; nine guys to take out one man? When I heard they were going to torture him, that's when everything changed for me. That's when I felt that I couldn't ignore it any longer. Everything pointed to Lombardo and everyone on the inside told me that it was Lombardo. It had become time for me to accept it and continue with my plans. Deep down, I knew there was no longer a question to it."

In 1997, Nick built himself a modified assault rifle with a high-power scope. It was assembled from parts of several different guns to avoid any chance of it being traced. His plan was simple: to take out the man that killed his father. He carefully made custom rounds especially for the risky task at hand; rounds that also couldn't be traced and whose noise would be low enough to be covered up by the noisy streets of a busy city such as Chicago. With nothing but enough cash for emergencies, he climbed on his motorcycle with the dismantled weapon and headed up to Chicago.

"I took my time," Nick recalls. "Lombardo was a neighborhood guy, and even though he was gone a lot, hiding here or there, he'd always come back to his home for a short time. I scoped out the place for a couple days and I went across the street and found a roof top that had a couple exit points as well as a short distance to the next roof. I grabbed some boards and spanned the gap in case I needed to get across to another building."

"Lombardo's house was just off the expressway, which happened to be near an interstate," he recalls. "It made an easy exit for me, and if anyone was after me, they'd never know if I was headed north to Wisconsin, south-east to Indiana, or if I had gone south back through Illinois. I parked my bike two blocks away and timed my exit so that I knew I could be on the expressway within a couple minutes of the hit."

Nick climbed to the roof top and waited. "Ironically, it was how well I planned it that changed everything," he says. "I was comfortable; I had plenty of time. When the day came and Lombardo walked out onto his steps, I took the time to watch him through the scope. He lit and smoked a cigarette and I watched the flame. I remember that I watched the ember fall off the end of it. Everything slowed down for me and details became completely clear. He was wearing glasses, and I slowly focused the cross hairs on the little shiny piece of metal that bridged the lenses. I figured a shot that was a little high would hit his forehead; a little low his face; a little to either side would hit his eyes. Any of those options would kill him."

It was during this time as he observed the man whom he had known as a child as "Uncle Joey" that Nick's mind began to churn with the impact of the effects of killing Lombardo. "I could only think of my son," he says as he remembers that moment.

"I was convinced I could get away with it, but there is always that small chance that something goes wrong. In this case, it would lead to jail or a hit on my family. I wanted to ensure that my son had what I didn't get the chance to experience; a life with a father."

Nick continued to watch Joey Lombardo through the scope until the man whom Nick had spent years hunting and investigating, the man responsible for the brutal murder of his father, walked away and out of sight. Sitting back and looking at the skyline of the city behind him, Nick felt a strange sense of confliction.

"For my family, I let him go. I spared him. At that moment, it just wasn't worth it to me. I walked the two blocks to my bike, got on and rode home to Florida," he recalls.

On February 2, 2009, after Joey "the Clown" Lombardo was sentenced for Danny's murder, Nick realized that the satisfying goal, the vengeful closure he had hoped for would not be his. Nick could only sit in the Federal courtroom watching Lombardo, now a broken-down old man, be sentenced to life in prison. His father's killer, no matter how ill or old he was, would still keep living.

"It was then that I realized Lombardo's conviction doesn't solve anything," Nick says. "Sure they finally put him away. But he got to live his whole life and provide millions of dollars to his family. He got to wake up in the morning, take a breath, and do all the things that my father didn't get a chance to. By killing my father, he took everything away from our family. I've survived but at what expense?"

Nick would often think of that moment when he had the man who killed his father focused in the cross hairs of his scope.

"I sometimes think that what I regret most to this day is not the fact that I didn't do it," Nick says, "but that I never let him know how close I was to doing it—that I could have done it—that his fucking head was just a trigger pull away from having a bullet hit it. And that the bullet would have come from Danny Seifert's son. That, most of all, is what I regret."

CHAPTER 14

Justice Unrealized

On July 27, 1998, exactly one year and two months before Emma and Joe had their private ceremony at Daniel's grave site to "bury the past," a letter was sent from the Milan, Michigan, Federal Correctional Institution to the FBI that would change the course of the Seiferts' lives and throw them once again into turmoil, pulling them back into their dark past.[47]

For the family as a whole, this turmoil would be an ironic blend of having to re-live and agonize over the events of that tragic

---

[47] US Department of Justice, Operation Family Secrets
http://www.justice.gov/usao/iln/hot/familySecrets.html#Jul10

day in 1974, while simultaneously experiencing a chance to realize a lifelong desire for justice. However, for Danny's two sons, it would also lead to utter deflation and would force Joe and Nick to each ruefully reconsider their earlier choices of not taking justice into their own hands.

The FBI opened a typed one-page note that simply read:

> "I am sending you this letter in total confidentiality. [...] IT [sic] is very important that you show or talk to nobody about this letter except who you have to. The less people that know I am contacting you the more I can and will help and be able to help you."[48]

The letter came from Frank Calabrese Jr., the son of Cicero, Illinois Mob boss Frank Calabrese Sr., and was sent in an effort to let the Feds know that Frank Jr., incarcerated since 1997, had decided to flip and was intent on cooperating with Federal investigators.

This cooperation on behalf of Frank Jr. stemmed ultimately from Frank's personal vendetta against his father's abuse, the latest of which resulted in Frank Jr. staring down the barrel of a gun after Frank Jr. had stolen hundreds of thousands of dollars from him. Sitting in jail and allowing the past to steep made Frank Jr. believe that his father truly didn't love him and was actually quite capable of

---

[48] US Department of Justice, Operation Family Secrets
http://www.justice.gov/usao/iln/hot/familySecrets.html#Jul10

killing him, even in jail. According to Frank Jr., this made him decided to open up to the FBI.

Echoing this fear of a possible jail hit, his letter to the Feds stated, "Please, if you decide to come make sure very few staff at MILAN know your reason for coming because if they do they might tell my father and that would be a danger to me."

Ultimately, this move by Frank Jr. would lead his uncle, Nicholas Calabrese (known for protecting Frank Jr.), to also open up to the feds. Together, the two veteran mobsters would drop a veritable treasure of Mob-related information straight into the hands of Federal investigators.

Not only was Frank Jr. intent on cooperating and testifying, but with his family ties to the Chicago Outfit, he was ready to enlighten the Feds and the public with inside information on prominent Chicago mobsters, including his father Frank Sr., as well as his uncle, Nick Calabrese. Frank Jr.'s revelations would also prove invaluable in shedding light upon multiple unsolved Mob-related murders including Danny Seifert's. But perhaps most importantly, Frank Jr. could also shed light on the violent rule of the Chicago Mafia from the perspective of an insider who not only knew all of the key players, but also the roles and responsibilities of those individuals.

Calabrese's desperate letter concluded with the words, "This is no game. I feel I have to help you get this sick man locked up forever."[49]

Spoken against his father, these words would become the key for the Seiferts and the general public to not only obtain an insider's vision of the events leading to the death of Danny, but would also prove a gateway for the Feds that would open the way to finally be able to "put a hit on the Mob,"[50] as US Attorney Patrick Fitzgerald would later state to the press.

The Feds quickly jumped at the opportunity to work with Frank Jr., and on Valentine's Day of 1999, just seven months shy of the 25th year anniversary of Danny's death, Frank Jr. began to secretly tape conversations he had with his father during visits for the FBI, while the two would walk around the prison yard.

But this would prove to be just the beginning. The tapes obtained from these secret conversations would outline a network of Mobsters linked to murder, corruption, the Chicago police department, and an intricate web of major criminal players. The complaint from the Department of Justice broke down how "the

---

[49] Warmbir, Steve. "The Letter that Started it All." Chicago Sun Times, August 23, 2007.
http://blogs.suntimes.com/mob/2007/08/the_letter_that_started_it_all.html#more

[50] Davey, Monica. "In Mob Sweep, Feds Hope to Send Up the Clown." The New York Times, April 26, 2005.
http://www.nytimes.com/2005/04/26/national/26mob.html?_r=0

organization allegedly employed intimidation, bribery, and murder to protect itself against witnesses and turncoats within its ranks."

Witnesses such as Danny Seifert, it became clear, were among those whom the Mob "protected" itself against. The indictments against Frank Sr. included specific charges of no less than ten murders. For his brother Nick, the indictment included "16 murders that Nicholas Calabrese was personally involved with." It also listed "22 other murders of which Nicholas Calabrese had second-hand knowledge."[51]

The sum of this evidence would lead to a huge Federal investigation code-named "Operation Family Secrets." Ultimately, this investigation would lead to the largest and most prominent Mob trial since Al Capone, The Family Secrets Trial. On Monday April 25, 2005, the Department of Justice released a press announcement regarding this investigation that read:

14 DEFENDANTS INDICTED FOR ALLEGED ORGANIZED CRIME ACTIVITIES; "CHICAGO OUTFIT" NAMED AS RICO ENTERPRISE IN FOUR-DECADE CONSPIRACY ALLEGING 18 MOB MURDERS AND 1 ATTEMPTED MURDER

---

[51] Operation Family Secrets Indictment (United States vs. Nicholas Calabrese, Joseph Marcello, Joseph Lombardo, et al), August 2003.
http://www.justice.gov/usao/iln/indict/2005/familySecrets.pdf

CHICAGO – Eighteen previously unsolved murders and one attempted murder – all between 1970 and 1986 in the Chicago area, except one slaying in Arizona – form the core of a racketeering conspiracy indictment spanning four decades that was unsealed today against 14 defendants.

The conspiracy allegedly extended from the mid-1960s to the present, and included the following murders and attempted murder:

- Michael Albergo, also known as "Hambone," in or about August, 1970, in Chicago;
- Daniel Seifert, on or about September 27, 1974, in Bensenville;
- Paul Haggerty, on or about June 24, 1976, in Chicago;
- Henry Cosentino, on or about March 15, 1977;
- John Mendell, on or about January 16, 1978, in Chicago;
- Donald Renno and Vincent Moretti, on or about January 31, 1978, in Cicero;
- William and Charlotte Dauber, on or about July 2, 1980, in Will County;
- William Petrocelli, on or about December 30, 1980, in Cicero;
- Michael Cagnoni, on or about June 24, 1981, in DuPage County;
- Nicholas D'Andrea, on or about September 13, 1981, in Chicago Heights;
- attempted murder of Individual A, on or about April 24, 1982, in Lake County;
- Richard D. Ortiz and Arthur Morawski, on or about July 23, 1983, in Cicero;
- Emil Vaci, on or about June 7, 1986, in Phoenix;
- Anthony and Michael Spilotro, on or about June 14, 1986, in DuPage County;

- John Fecarotta, on or about September 14, 1986, in Chicago.

While these arrests will have a significant and long-term effect on the operations of the Outfit, it does not signal the end of their reign in Chicago. We will continue with our efforts to eradicate what has been one of the most prolific organized crime enterprises in the United States.

Seven of the 11 defendants charged in the racketeering conspiracy count allegedly committed murder or agreed to commit murder on the Outfit's behalf. All 11 defendants in that count allegedly engaged in such other illegal activities as collecting "street tax;" illegal gambling businesses involving sports bookmaking and video gambling machines; collecting debts incurred in the illegal gambling businesses; making usurious "juice loans;" using extortion, threats, violence and intimidation to collect juice loan and other debts, obstructing justice; and traveling interstate to further the goals of the Outfit. The three defendants not charged in the racketeering conspiracy are charged in other counts of the indictment with illegal gambling and/or tax fraud conspiracy.

The following defendants were being arrested this morning in Illinois: **James Marcello**, 63, of Lombard; **Joseph Lombardo**, 75, of Chicago; **Michael Marcello**, 55, of Schaumburg; **Nicholas Ferriola**, 29, of Westchester; **Joseph Venezia**, 62, of Hillside; **Thomas Johnson**, 49, of Willow Springs; and his nephew, **Dennis Johnson**, 34, of Lombard. The deceased defendant, **Frank Saladino**, 59, of Hampshire and formerly of Freeport and Rockford, was discovered dead in a hotel room where he was living in Hampshire in Kane County; Another defendant, **Michael Ricci**, 75, of Streamwood, was expected to voluntarily surrender to the FBI. Those defendants in custody were expected to appear at 2 p.m. today before U.S. District Court Judge James Zagel in Chicago.

Two defendants, **Frank Schweihs**, 75, of Dania, Fla., and formerly of Chicago, and **Anthony Doyle**, 60, of Wickenburg,

Ariz., and formerly of Chicago, were being arrested in Florida and Arizona, respectively, and are expected to have court appearances today in Ft. Lauderdale and Phoenix.

Three defendants, **Nicholas W. Calabrese**, 62, of Chicago; his brother, **Frank Calabrese, Sr.**, 68, of Oak Brook; and **Paul Schiro**, 67, of Phoenix, were already in federal custody. They will appear on dates to be determined later in Federal Court in Chicago.[52]

The unprecedented indictment also offered an overview of the Outfit's structure and chain of command, and detailed how its criminal activities were carried out by six main "crews" that were broken down by their geographic locations in the Chicago metropolitan area. These included the Elmwood Park; the North Side/Rush Street; the South Side/26th Street (Chinatown); Grand Avenue; Melrose Park; and the Chicago Heights crew.

Each Chicago Outfit crew, the indictment asserted, was run by a leader known as a street boss or "Capo." Joey "the Clown" Lombardo for instance, allegedly was and remained the Capo for the Grand Avenue crew. Someone who proved himself useful and criminally trustworthy was given special "made" status in the Outfit. But a mobster could not normally be "made" unless he was of Italian descent and had committed at least one murder on behalf of the

---

[52] Operation Family Secrets Indictment (United States vs. Nicholas Calabrese, Joseph Marcello, Joseph Lombardo, et al), August 2003.
http://www.justice.gov/usao/iln/indict/2005/familySecrets.pdf

Outfit. Someone who sought to gain this coveted "made" status also had to be sponsored by his Capo.

The "making" of a mobster culminated in a much-speculated-upon ceremony in which the person to be "made" was commanded to swear allegiance to the Mob enterprise. Practically the stuff of legend, no one on the outside of the Mob had ever seen this ceremony; let alone listen to an insider describe details of it. Yet this ceremony would be described in full detail by Nicholas Calabrese, who admitted that he and his brother Frank Sr. were "made" during a ceremony in 1983. Once made, the mobster was then sworn into the Outfit to serve for life and had to vow that the Outfit would come first before anything in that individual's life—even above family.

The Federal prosecution's activity that stemmed from the willingness of Frank Jr. and Nick Calabrese to cooperate with the FBI, ultimately led to a phone call in 2003 to Emma Seifert from the FBI. As a stunned and distrustful Emma listened, the Agent said he was calling to inform her that because of new evidence, the FBI was once again picking up the investigation into her husband's death.

"I told him to go to hell and hung up the phone," Emma recalls of her reaction to the news of the renewed investigations. "I didn't want to relive it all over again, and I didn't know what it would do to the kids. All I knew is that it had been so long, and we had come so far as a family. Suddenly I was right back in September of 1974. I just couldn't handle it and I immediately called Joe."

At first the Seiferts thought that the reopening of their case would finally lead to some answers. For their whole lives, they had known in their hearts what exactly had happened that day, but they had never been able to prove it. At last, they felt that Lombardo would finally get arrested, charged, and be tried for the murder, and would finally have to defend himself for his actions that day. For the first time in thirty years, the Seiferts would have a chance to be in the same room with the reputed Mob boss and the one-time family patron whom they knew deep down was responsible for the death of Danny.

"We felt and hoped that we might get some closure," Joe recalls about the day when his mother informed him of Danny's case being reopened.

"Mom was very upset about it, but my first reaction was, 'No shit? That's awesome!' She wasn't at all happy with my response, but I wanted to see this guy on the stand defending himself. I wanted to see him talk about the murder and talk about our family. And I wanted to look him in the eye as he did it."

Emma felt she was once again about to enter another very difficult time in her life, and that the trial was just the start of even more bad things to come. Her current husband, Ed, had been diagnosed with cancer in 2003, and the couple both had been battling very difficult health problems. She was frail both emotionally and physically, and Emma knew that the trial would take a large psychological toll on everyone in her family, especially herself. She wasn't sure if she could hold up during the trial or not, and deep down she just wanted it all to go away once and for all.

On September 2, 2004, Emma was called before the Grand Jury to testify as a witness to Danny's death. The questioning was administered by Assistant US Attorneys John Scully and Mitchell Mars, both of whom were specialists who worked in the Organized Crime division of the US Attorney's office. During the interview, she recalled details of the actions and behaviors of members of International Fiberglass, including Felix "Milwaukee Phil" Alderisio, Irwin Weiner, and Joseph Lombardo, as well as Ronald DeAngelis and Harold Lurie. She discussed how she knew that Danny also knew Tony "the Ant" Spilotro, because Danny used to talk to her about him all the time.

She continued by describing the falling out between Danny and Joey Lombardo, when Lombardo had claimed that Danny owed him $5,000 upon leaving International, as a payback for the initial investment that the others in the firm had originally put up. She also recalled that Danny had been threatened by "his old partners at International Fiberglass on several occasions" after he started another company with his uncle.

"These threats had forced us to close the company," Emma testified, "because Danny's uncle was intimidated by Danny's former partners."

This in turn, led to the formation of Plasti-Matic Products in Bensenville, by Danny and Emma.

Emma openly discussed Danny's focus on security for the family as well as his ownership of approximately a dozen firearms scattered throughout the house and company. She recalled for the Grand Jury how the threats to Danny in 1973 had increased, and she also recalled the events of Danny's last days that were tied to Lombardo.

Approximately one to two weeks prior to the murder [...] Daniel told me of a telephone conversation and a visit to his office of Plasti-Matic Products by Lombardo. Over the phone, Lombardo indicated that he was having some technical problems of some nature at International Fiberglass and wanted to talk to Daniel. Lombardo visited Plasti-Matic Products later that day and was given a tour of the premises by Danny. Lombardo was accompanied by his girlfriend, Bonnie Vent. Later in the evening, when describing the visit to me, he indicated that Joey seemed like he wanted to talk about something but wouldn't. Daniel felt very uncomfortable about the visit and believed that the reasons Lombardo gave for the visit to Plasti-Matic were pure fiction.

When Emma discussed the day of the murder, she stated that she initially thought Danny might have reached safety because she last saw him "running east through the parking lot," but eventually she discovered her husband had been slain. She noted that Danny always had kept at least two handguns at the factory, one in the drawer which she retrieved during that day, and another in the warehouse section of the building where the assassins had been hiding. After the murder, it was discovered that this gun was missing, leading her to believe that the killers had searched the factory for weapons before she and Danny had arrived later that morning.

She concluded her testimony with a final chilling piece of information. "A few weeks after Daniel's murder, Lombardo contacted me over the telephone claiming he wanted to retrieve some paperwork. I felt the phone call was of a threatening nature, even though no direct threats were made. I informed Lombardo that any paperwork that was previously located in Plasti-Matic Products was now in the possession of the FBI. I never spoke to Lombardo again."

Just two weeks before Emma's testimony to the Grand Jury, she had an experience that brought her right back to those early days of terror and intimidation.

"We had already gone back to living on constant edge," Emma recalls of the incident. "Ed and I, based on the urging of Joe, had installed an alarm in our house with video cameras to see anyone who approached the property. I had also gotten my pistol back from my sister Judy, just in case."

She continues, "One morning at 4:30am, two weeks before my testimony, someone rang our doorbell. I was supposed to be leaving at 4:30am with my sister Virginia that morning, to go see my brother who was very ill. But she had cancelled the night before. At first I thought she had come by anyway, even though I wasn't ready. But when I looked out the window, there was a man standing across the street near an SUV, staring at our house and smoking a cigarette. He was dressed in dark clothes, and I couldn't make out his face. I told Ed who ran downstairs with the gun to get a better look. In that time, the man flicked the cigarette at our house and drove off. I couldn't get a license plate number, and by time Ed opened the garage door, he was gone. I had no idea who he was, and what was frightening was that he showed up right at the time I was supposed to be leaving. If my sister hadn't cancelled, I don't know what would have happened."

Emma carefully picked up the cigarette and placed it in a plastic bag, and Joe immediately called the FBI who later tried to run prints off of the cigarette, but to no avail. The man was never seen again. But it stands out in the minds of Joe and Emma as yet another instance of how close these people are, and how this family will never know for sure if an event such as this is coincidence, or something more sinister.

"For twenty years, I had gotten to the point of living an almost-normal life," Emma says. "But the trial, which was supposed to bring closure, ended that for me. Ironically, it brought everything back, and all of us are back on edge just as we were decades ago; perhaps even more so, with Nick and Joe."

Lombardo was finally indicted on April 25, 2005 in the culmination of Operation Family Secrets and would be on the run from the FBI for almost nine months, until his arrest in January 2006.

Tony Spilotro's brother, Pat, is the person who is credited for tipping the Feds to the whereabouts of Joey Lombardo when he was on the run, enabling is capture. Lombardo had earlier arranged to come into Pat's dental office with an abscessed tooth. Unbeknownst to Lombardo at the time, Pat Spilotro was actually working with the FBI to set up Lombardo. While there, Pat had questioned Lombardo about the details of his two brothers' (Tony and Michael) deaths. The response to Pat's question was clear as Lombardo allegedly replied, "Doc, you get an order, you follow that order. If you don't follow the order, you go too."[53]

Confirming that Lombardo was directly responsible for the killing of his two brothers, Pat contacted the Feds and informed them of Lombardo's whereabouts. Lombardo was then captured at

---

[53] Coen, Jeff. "How Dentist's Tip Led to Lombardo's Arrest." *Chicago Tribune*, August 08, 2007.
http://articles.chicagotribune.com/2007-08-08/news/0708071148_1_michael-spilotro-lombardo-rick-halprin

the house of one of his friends and would sit in prison until the start of the Family Secrets trial in June of 2007.

During this emotional and difficult time for Emma, she received some unexpected good news that would help to balance the arduous trial ahead. She would finally come to realize a dream-come-true for her when she was contacted by an adoption agency and informed that the child she had given up so many years ago wanted to reconnect with her. Until this time, Emma hadn't even realized that the baby she had given birth to years ago was a girl.

"I didn't know what to say," she recalls. "It came out of nowhere and suddenly I felt that this piece of me that had been lost so long ago was near. I felt like a breath of life had been given to me."

The process was supposed to take quite a while before the two were able to meet, but luckily, Emma happened to tell Joe about the situation. He asked for the daughter's name, the agency's name, and by using his own contacts was able to track Emma's daughter down in only a day.

"Sometimes it's good to be connected," Joe jokingly said to his mom when he gave her the information.

Once the trial began, the Seiferts came together as a family in a way that, ironically, they hadn't been able to do since Danny's death. Besides her daughter's reuniting with Emma, Joe had also reconnected with Nick after a separation of many years. As the two brothers shared stories of their more recent lives, they both realized that strong bond between them wasn't as far off as each had thought.

"Besides needing to be away from Chicago for my own piece of mind, I also moved away to protect my family from my own investigations," Nick recalls. "I knew that some of the people that I contacted would not be happy about it, and I felt it best to be as far away from mom and Joe as possible, to prevent any blowback onto them. I was trying to make waves, and I didn't care who knew about it; the Mob, the FBI, whoever. So it could have been dangerous for them at times. But they were always on my mind, and I missed both of them more than I can say."

A few weeks into the trial, Joe became an expert at funneling reporters' requests to interview him and couldn't help but laugh whenever he saw himself on the evening news. However, while Joe enjoyed the brief attention as a way to shed public light onto Lombardo, the trial was also something very serious to everyone in their family, especially for Joe. He was not only there that day when Lombardo killed his father; he was even named after the very man who everyone felt was directly responsible for the murder. Joe had a lifetime of questions, anger, and inner demons to try and somehow resolve, and with the trial, everything resurfaced for him to deal with all at once. Even when the rest of the family had wanted to move on, Joe never would or could, at least not as fully as his family attempted to do. He saw this trial as a final opportunity to not only

239

see justice done to Lombardo, but also as an opportunity to connect on some level with his father, the man whom he lost thirty years before.

In preparation for the trial, Joe took some steps to ensure that Lombardo would know exactly who he was when he was inside the courtroom. Joe's wife Julie noted that "he wore his dad's gold watch throughout the trial" in homage to his father. Joe also made it a point to lose twenty-five pounds before the trial in order to be thin and lean like his father had been. He cut his hair in the same style that his father had worn, and grew his goatee to look exactly the same. There were times during the trial that even Emma would be startled by how close the resemblance was.

"I remember one day Joe standing on the stairs in our home, and it was as if I had flashed back thirty years and was looking at Danny," she recalls.

Emma would not be the only one to notice either. Joe made it a point to sit in the front of the courtroom when Lombardo was there, always up close. He would stare coldly and unflinchingly at the veteran mobster.

Once during the trial, Robert T. York, a retired FBI Agent left the stand and was walking by the family seating area and saw Joe. The retired agent looked right into Joe's eyes, stopped walking, looked at him again stunned, and then finally continued on. Noting

York's reaction, Julie recalls, "It was as if he was seeing Danny all over again."

The trial also gave Joe a chance to listen to people's assessments of his father. Alva Johnson Rogers, a witness in the Federal Witness Protection Program who heard Lombardo discuss Danny's murder a day later in 1974, relayed a message to Joe and Nick through the US Attorney's Victim's coordinator. Rogers told her to tell them "their father was a good guy, not like the rest of them. That Rogers knew and liked their dad and felt bad when listening to Lombardo describe the murder the next day at the golf course."

Joe also got to see his uncle, Bob, whom he hadn't seen since he was a child. As Bob testified in court how Lombardo had told him just before the murder, "'[You] better straighten Danny out, or you know what's going to happen to him,'" Julie noted Joe's noticeable reaction to Bob in her journal. She wrote, "It felt like a piece of his father was up there through his uncle, because Joe didn't have many memories of his dad."

For his family, it was clear to everyone that Joe was desperately trying to feel every single connection to his father that he could find. The trial would be his one and final chance to do so. Even on this diminished and tragic level, it was something that he had missed out for his entire life. To Joe, it was a fleeting chance to experience being father and son, and in some ways, helping to defend his father, which he couldn't do so many years ago.

The family listened to Lombardo as he described his relationship with Danny, having "learned everything I know about fiberglass from him." In a deep, rough voice, Lombardo then denied being part of the masked, armed hit-men that ambushed Danny at Plasti-Matic thirty years ago, beating and killing him as Joe and Emma stared helplessly in horror.

"I'm sorry for their loss then; I'm sorry for their loss now," Lombardo told the courtroom. He even addressed Nick as "Nicky," perhaps subconsciously invoking the relationship he had with Danny's oldest son decades ago.

During the trial, Lombardo denied having been a member of the Mob, let alone a "made" member, and only admitted to running low-level street gambling games and pitching pennies as a little kid. Lombardo's lawyer, Rick Halprin, even acknowledged that Lombardo "Ran the oldest and most reliable floating craps game on Grand Avenue."

Joey "the Clown" Lombardo, is one of the last old-school Chicago mobsters. With his commonly known antics such as hiding behind a newspaper with a hole cut in it, he became an almost cliché representation of organized crime and he'll deny everything until the very end, even if they have pictures. Even a well-known image known as "The Last Supper" of Lombardo with aging Mob leaders snapped in a Chicago restaurant (Government Photo Exhibit #1 in the Family Secrets Trial)[54], Lombardo insisted he was just there to pick up a sandwich and not part of the group of men who were photographed.

However, what Lombardo didn't realize is that besides pictures, the Feds had transcripts of Lombardo on their wire taps. In particular, one set of transcripts from 1979 stood out during the trial as the prosecution attempted to show Lombardo's true Mob persona. These transcripts demonstrated Lombardo's role and power, his connection to Allen Dorfman, the Teamsters, and Jimmy Hoffa, as well as his potential for lethality as he paid a visit to Morris Shenker, a lawyer and associate of Allen Dorfman who happened to owe the Mob (i.e., "the system" as Lombardo refers to it in the transcript) some money. At the end of the dialogue, Lombardo's warning to Shenker couldn't be clearer.

Date: 05/22/1979
Place: AIA OFFICES
Activity: Title III Intercept

SPEAKERS:
    DORFMAN: Allen Dorfman
    SHENKER: Morris Shenker
    LOMBARDO: Joseph Lombardo

---

[54] US Department of Justice, Operation Family Secrets
http://www.justice.gov/usao/iln/hot/familySecrets.html#Jul10

LOMBARDO:	Morris, the the reason why I'm here, you don't know who I am.
SHENKER:	I'm...
LOMBARDO:	My name is Joey.
SHENKER:	I'm, I'm assuming you're all right, if you're with Allen.
LOMBARDO:	That's right. That's right. Okay. Here's the reason why.
SHENKER:	(UI)
LOMBARDO:	Allen belongs to Chicago. Now you know what I mean when he belongs to Chicago? I was sent here to find out what the story is. When they talk to Allen, he says he don't get this, he don't *get* this, he got this, he got this coming. It's 12 years - they're tired of listening to this bullshit, that he don't have this and Morris is this and Morris is that.
SHENKER:	Okay, you...
LOMBARDO:	You know where you belong, I mean, excuse me, you know where you belong, and he knows where he belongs and the other guy knows where he belongs - we all belong to certain people, to account to - it's a big world. And that's what I'm here for is to listen. And the word is that Morris says this and Morris says that, Morris says...and that's why I say, now what you say you got coming, you don't got coming...now you're here. According to what I see...hear you say.
SHENKER:	Never did to IJK, Nevada?

LOMBARDO:	Now it's getting to the point now where you either gonna shit or get off the pot, ya know what I mean? We either get what we got coming or we don't get what we got coming.
SHENKER:	Well.
LOMBARDO:	If we got something coming we want it. If we don't have it coming, we don't want it.
SHENKER:	Well, I, I can only tell you what he has coming (UI).
LOMBARDO:	Good. Well, I, what he's got coming, the people in Chicago got coming.
SHENKER:	Well that's between you fellas.
LOMBARDO:	I know that, dick.
SHENKER:	You know what I mean, but, I can tell you what, what, ah, what, what happened is that IJK, Nevada was never involved in any of this. If you'd recall that came way later. IJK, Nevada didn't come until 1972, 73, and I can tell you who had the money, who put the money up, how the money was put up. It has absolutely nothing to do with Penasquitos. Not this much.
LOMBARDO:	Well, that's up to the people here to decide. Ya know what I mean? You have to find a way to pay it. They'll decide what to do. I'm just go back with the message...I just...
SHENKER:	No one is telling me what to do. I never did business with them. Let me tell you something.
LOMBARDO:	What?

SHENKER:	You know, I'm the nicest guy in the world, but on the other hand, nobody is going to make me do anything. I never did business with them.
LOMBARDO:	That's true.
SHENKER:	I did business with Hoffa...(UI)
LOMBARDO:	That's true.
SHENKER:	I did business with Hoffa and Hoffa said you and they know? And that's it.
LOMBARDO:	But Morris, I'm just. I'm just here to listen to it and bring back...
SHENKER:	...(UI)
LOMBARDO:	Excuse me. I'm just here to bring a message back. And what I think is what and what's, what and let me tell you something. If they make a decision and they tell me to come back and bring you a message to pay, you can fight the system if you wanna, but, I'll tell you one thing. You say you're 72, and you defy it, all you can do is send a guy like me to jail, one guy.
SHENKER:	I'm not going to send anybody to jail.
LOMBARDO:	But, excuse me, but you ain't gonna send the system to jail.
SHENKER:	I'm not going to send anybody to jail.
LOMBARDO:	I'm just tellin' ya. I'm just tellin' ya (raising his voice). If they come back and tell me to give you a message and if you defy it, I assure you that you will never reach 73.[55]

---

[55] US Department of Justice, Operation Family Secrets
http://www.justice.gov/usao/iln/hot/familySecrets.html#Jul10

Lombardo disputed what he said to Shenker in this dialogue as simply "playing a role" as a mobster and not really being a mobster, in order to try and intimidate Shenker to pay his money by using the tool of fear. In the end, these transcripts were a final brush stroke for the prosecution's painting of Joey Lombardo's true Mob character to the jury.

Thirty-three years to the day of Danny's death, on September 27, 2007, Joey "the Clown" Lombardo was found guilty of the murder of Danny Seifert. However, because of legal stall tactics, it would take several months of enduring procedural legal games on the part of Lombardo's flamboyant attorney Rick Halprin, until the Seiferts would finally see Lombardo sentenced.

On February 2, 2009, Federal Judge Zagel arranged the sentencing for Lombardo. The once-feared mobster arrived to court seated in a wheelchair and wearing an orange prison jumpsuit. A mere shadow of the man he used to be, but still powerful nonetheless. Joe Seifert took this opportunity to address Lombardo directly just prior to the sentencing, and wrote the following for his speech:

I can't believe it's been over thirty years. Time has passed so quickly I'm really not sure how to write or where to begin. I am here to present my long fatherless life. I've lived through some of the most important times in a child's life, especially a young boy's life. I would love to present to you every instance that I had trouble coping with since my father's murder, but we'd be here for weeks.

Joe continued to describe his perspective of the events of that day in 1974, notably with the inner recollection of a four-year-old child.

I was playing sick and gonna go to work with my parents and play with my toys! I never did get to play with my cars that day, instead I watched frozen in the middle of chaos as men viciously beat and shot my father in the front of the office. Blood splattered the walls and the floor the last time I remember seeing my father I was sitting in the back of a car. It was sunny out and he was laying [sic] twisted in the grass. As I think about that image today, I wonder if I ever said goodbye. I was told at the wake that I wanted to say goodbye but I didn't know who the person was in the casket...it didn't look like my father at all. I will never forget those few days following the murder; it was my first true taste of grief.

He had shortened his statement from the original version, and removed the discussion of anger, rage, and a ruined life. Instead, Joe ended it with a simple, emotional summary of the reason that so many people had worked so hard for over thirty years, and pointed out the most fundamental reason for the Family Secrets trial.

Lastly, we should remember that this day is not about Joe Lombardo or what I have to say or not say, it's about remembering a friend, a brother, a husband, and most importantly, my father, Daniel Raymond Seifert, and for his voice to be heard. Thank you.

After the family's statements were read, Federal Judge Zagel spoke to Joey Lombardo directly.

"Mr. Lombardo, you are not like the toxic creature I've seen forming in one of your co-defendants," Zagel told Lombardo, referring to Frank Calabrese, Sr., whom Zagel had sentenced to life in prison only one week prior to Lombardo's sentencing.

"You evidence some balance and judgment and based on the evidence before me, some ability to charm people. In the end, we are judged by our actions and not on our wit or our smiles...In cases like these, the things that matter most are the worst things we do. The worst things you have done are terrible, and I see no regret in you. I think you felt you were engaged in a game in which you drew satisfaction in how you played the game...it wasn't a game, and it involved the destruction of a human life."

Judge Zagel then sentenced Joey "the Clown" Lombardo to life in prison for the convictions[56], and sentenced him separately to

---

[56] "Joey the Clown Lombardo Sentenced to Life." *NBC Chicago / Associated Press*, February 2, 2009.
http://www.nbcchicago.com/news/local/Joey-The-Clown-Lombardo-Sentenced-to-Life.html

168 months in prison for being on the run for eight months after he was charged. The gavel slammed, closing the final chapter of Lombardo's criminal life and silencing at least some of the ghosts that had plagued the Seiferts for so long.

With the sentencing over and a rush of reporters swarming the family with questions, the search for justice was finally over for the Seiferts. Yet, while some family members admit that they did feel a sense of closure, it was not at all what they expected. As one reporter moved in close to the family as they walked away from the courthouse, he asked Joe the simple question, "Was justice done today?"

Joe looked at the man, paused, and replied with an empty realization, "There is no justice."

Nick and Joe walked away from the reporters, climbed into a waiting SUV and drove off. Both were quiet. Joe turned and looked at Nick and the two brothers had mutual recognition in their eyes for what each was thinking.

"I should have fucking done it when I had the chance," Nick told his brother.

Joe turned around silently, reached under the seat and stuck the hidden .45, just like the one his father carried, into his waistband. Danny's two sons, each lost in their own thoughts, watched with vacant eyes as the buildings of Chicago passed by them in a blur of cold grey.

The next day, the two brothers paid a quiet, solemn visit to their father's grave in what was supposed to be a moment of triumph. Standing in the biting February cold under a large Pine tree that shadows the grave site, the two men stared in silence at the tombstone. They knew this moment wouldn't be the end of their pain.

The next day Nick would fly back to Florida to a life unchanged. The feeling of closure that he and his family had searched decades for, was unrealized. He had told the courtroom during the trial, "I felt like a coward for many years for not seeking revenge for what those men did to my father."

While the jury had no idea of his aborted plan of retribution, deep down, he knew he wasn't a coward; that he *could* have done it. What he labeled as "cowardly" to the courtroom, was really a deep personal regret that he would have to learn to live with the rest of his life. Only by looking at his own children each day as they grow up with a father, does Nick keep his regret in check.

Emma silently carries the burden of these decades with a new realization regarding the futility of everything that surrounds her husband's murder.

"I'll never have closure," she says regretfully, regarding the Family Secrets Trial. "I know that now. I have so much buried inside me, so many things that I can never speak of, just for my own sanity. I truly hoped this trial would help me and my family to find some level of peace, but it won't. It can't. Nothing can."

Joe would continue to wrestle with the demons born of that day and face the realization that his life and family was still being torn apart on many levels, due to his father's murder so many years ago. Ironically, the trial put a final, irrevocable strain on his marriage, forcing the end to another relationship in Joe's life. While he realized some level of victory with Lombardo's conviction, he had lost yet another element of his life that was dear to him. In a June 2007 interview for the *Chicago Sun Times*, Joe stated that the murder of his father had created a "monster" inside of his family. From the moment of his father's murder, Joe would come to find that this "monster" would continue to relentlessly torment each of them for many years to come. For the Seiferts, true justice is something they would never be able to realize.

SOURCES

Interviews

John Drummond, Judy LaRue, Emma Seifert, Nick Seifert, Joe Seifert

Our sincere thanks to Mr. Drummond as well as to all the others who prefer to remain anonymous.

Government Documents/Reports

Affidavit. Statement to IRS by Daniel R. Seifert. May, 9, 1973.

Affidavit. Peter J. Wacks. Investigation of Rosemont, Illinois, Donald A. Stephens, and ties to organized crime.
http://www.ipsn.org/rosemont/wacks_affidavit_stephens.htm

FBI Interview, Emma Seifert, October 8, 1974.
http://blogs.suntimes.com/mob/2009/01/emma_seifert_fbi_interview.html

JFK Subcommittee Hearing, Executive Session, House of Representatives, May, 18, 1978.

Operation Family Secrets Indictment (United States vs. Nicholas Calabrese, Joseph Marcello, Joseph Lombardo, et al), August 2003.
http://www.justice.gov/usao/iln/indict/2005/familySecrets.pdf

Police Report. Bensenville, Illinois, December 13, 1972.

Trial Evidence

*NOTE: At time of printing, some files associated with previous administrations have been or will be moved to the Archive section of the Department Website, www.justice.gov.

US Department of Justice, Operation Family Secrets
http://www.justice.gov/usao/iln/hot/familySecrets.html#Jul10

Books and Periodicals

Balsamo, William and George Carpozi, Jr. *Crime Incorporated: The Inside Story of the Mafia's First 100 Years*. Fair Hills NJ: New Horizon Press, 1991.

Cain, Michael J. *The Tangled Web*. New York: Skyhorse, 2007.

Calabrese, Frank Jr., et al. *Operation Family Secrets: How a Mobster's Son and the FBI Brought Down Chicago's Murderous Crime Family*. NY: Random House, 2011.

Coen, Jeff. *Family Secrets: The Case that Crippled the Chicago Mob*. Chicago: Chicago Review Press, 2009.

Cohen, Adam, and Elizabeth Taylor. *American Pharaoh: Mayor Richard J. Daley: His Battle for Chicago and the Nation*. Boston: Little, Brown, and Company, 2000.

Cooley, Robert and Hillel Levin. *When Corruption was King*. New York: Carroll and Graf, 2004.

Corbit, Michael and Sam Giancana. *Double Deal*. New York: Harper Collins, 2003.

Deuchler, Douglas. *Cicero Revisited*. Chicago: Arcadia 2006.

Giancana, Sam and Scott M. Burnstein. *Family Affair. Treachery, Greed, and Betrayal in the Chicago Mafia*. New York: Berkley Books, 2010.

Roemer, William F. Jr. Accardo: The Genuine Godfather. New York: Ivy Books, 1995.

—. *The Enforcer - Spilotro: The Chicago Mob's Man over Las Vegas*. New York: Ivy Books, 1995.

Russo, Gus. *The Outfit: The Role of Chicago's Underworld in the Shaping of Modern America*. New York: Bloomsbury, 2004.

Court Filings and Transcripts

*NOTE: At time of printing, some files associated with previous administrations have been or will be moved to the Archive section of the Department Website, www.justice.gov.

Daily Herald, Stephens Mob Met in 1999, by Rob Olmstead
http://www.ipsn.org/rosemont/stephens_mob_met_in_1999.htm

Intercept between Joey Lombardo and Allen Dorfman
http://www.justice.gov/usao/iln/hot/familySecrets/2007_06_27/may_22_1979_t1.pdf

Intercept between Joey Lombardo, Allen Dorfman, and Morris Shenker
http://www.justice.gov/usao/iln/hot/familySecrets/2007_06_27/may_22_1979_t2.pdf

Intercept between Joey Lombardo and Louie Eboli
http://www.justice.gov/usao/iln/hot/familySecrets/2007_06_27/april_16_1979_t.pdf

Intercept between Anthony Spilotro, Joseph Hansen, and Frank Schweihs
http://www.justice.gov/usao/iln/hot/familySecrets/2007_06_27/may_8_1978_t.pdf

Operation Family Secrets Indictment
http://www.justice.gov/usao/iln/indict/2007/us_v_calabrese_etal_third.pdf

Operation Family Secrets Press Release
http://www.justice.gov/usao/iln/pr/chicago/2005/pr0425_01.pdf

Pete Wacks Affidavit
http://www.ipsn.org/rosemont/wacks_affidavit_stephens.htm

United States v. Dorfman. 1982 Indictment.
http://www.leagle.com/xmlResult.aspx?xmldoc=1982887542FSupp345_1825.xml&docbase=CSLWAR1-1950-1985

Articles

"Bring Your Own." *The Ledger*, May 16, 1973. http://news.google.com/newspapers?nid=1346&dat=1973051 6&id=d4ROAAAAIBAJ&sjid=cvoDAAAAIBAJ&pg=5977,44 40055

Buchthal, Kristina. "State Criticizes Rosemont Probe." *Crain's Chicago Business*, September 15, 2004. http://www.chicagobusiness.com/article/20040915/NEWS02 /200013909

Chase, John. "FBI Links Emerald Casino, Mob, and Mayor of Rosemont, Illinois." *Chicago Tribune*, July 19, 2005. http://articles.chicagotribune.com/2005-07-19/news/0507190223_1_illinois-gaming-board-rosemont-mob

"Chronological Order of La Cosa Nostra in the United States." The Nevada Observer, January 8, 2006. http://www.nevadaobserver.com/Chronological%20History% 20of%20La%20Cosa%20Nostra%20%281988%29.htm

Coen, Jeff. "Bookie Refuses to Bet on Mob." *Chicago Tribune*, July 03, 2007. http://articles.chicagotribune.com/2007-07-03/news/0707020813_1_testify-mob-joel-glickman

—. "How Dentist's Tip Led to Lombardo's Arrest." *Chicago Tribune*, August 08, 2007. http://articles.chicagotribune.com/2007-08-08/news/0708071148_1_michael-spilotro-lombardo-rick-halprin

"Crawling in the Gutter." Better Government Association, December 14, 2012. http://www.bettergov.org/crawling_in_the_gutter/

"Crime in America. How the Mob Controls Chicago." *The Saturday Evening Post*, November 1963.

Davey, Monica. "In Mob Sweep, Feds Hope to Send Up the Clown." The New York Times, April 26, 2005. http://www.nytimes.com/2005/04/26/national/26mob.html? _r=0

"DOJ press release on Major Indictment of Organized Crime Figures." Organized Crime and Political Corruption, April 25, 2005.
http://www.ipsn.org/indictments/indictments-oc/pr042505-outfit.htm

"Executive Session Testimony before the House Select Committee on Assassinations - Irwin Weiner."
http://jfkassassination.net/russ/m_j_russ/weiner.htm

Fusco, Chris. "Gaming Board bans Trash Firm over Family Ties / The Mob in Plainfield." The Plainfield Forum, December 23, 2002. http://www.topix.com/forum/city/plainfield-il/TKE1CU16HIL59BPSB

— "Rosemont Mayor Returns Mob-Linked Funds." *Chicago Sun Times*, 2008.
http://www.bettergov.org/rosemont_mayor_returns_mob-linked_funds/

Gerth, Jeff. "Richard M. Nixon and Organized Crime." *Penthouse*, July, 1974.
http://jfk.hood.edu/Collection/Weisberg%20Subject%20Index%20Files/N%20Disk/Nixon%20Richard%20M%20President%20Watergate%20Files/72-11-01%20Sundance%20Nixon%20and%20the%20Mafia/Item%2002.pdf

Havens, Jeff. "Reputed Mob Associate Bought Local Restaurant, Land." The Rock River Times, July, 2005
http://rockrivertimes.com/1993/07/01/reputed-mob-associate-bought-local-restaurant-land/

"I Didn't Do It." *Chicago Sun Times*, August 14, 2007.
http://www.suntimes.com/news/mob/510132,14mob.stng

"Illinois Police and Sheriff's News." *Organized Crime and Political Corruption*, 2006.
http://www.ipsn.org/wacks.htm

"Inside Story of Meeting to Free Giancana." *Chicago Tribune*, January 16, 1964.

"Investigation of Public Corruption." *Federal Bureau of Investigation,* March 2004.
http://www.fbi.gov/news/stories/2004/march/greylord_031504

"Is John DiFronzo Now the Undisputed Boss of the Chicago Mob?" The Chicago Syndicate, March 14, 2009.
http://www.thechicagosyndicate.com/2009/03/is-john-difronzo-now-undisputed-boss-of.html

"Joseph Lombardo." La Cosa Nostra Database.
http://www.lacndb.com/php/Info.php?name=Joseph%20Lombardo

"Joey the Clown Lombardo Sentenced to Life." NBC Chicago / Associated Press, February 2, 2009.
http://www.nbcchicago.com/news/local/Joey-The-Clown-Lombardo-Sentenced-to-Life.html

Jurvis, Rick and Liam Ford. "Grand Jury Lifting Veil on Unsolved Mob Hits." *Chicago Tribune,* January 23, 2005.

"Madigan Alleges Casino Mob Ties." *Chicago Sun Times,* March 26, 2004.
http://www.ipsn.org/rosemont/madigan_alleges_casino_mob_ties.htm

Malcolm, Andrew H. "Dorfman, Teamster Advisor Slain; Faced Long Term Bribery Case." *New York Times,* January 21, 1983.
http://www.nytimes.com/1983/01/21/us/dorfman-teamster-adviser-slain-faced-long-term-bribery-case.html

Moldea, Dan A. *The Hoffa Wars. The Rise and Fall of Jimmy Hoffa.* Paddington Press. 1978. (Online)
http://www.moldea.com/guerrilla.html#TheWorks

O'Brien, John. "Retiring FBI Agent Recalls Bugging Hole in Teamsters Case." *Chicago Tribune,* March 31, 1997.
http://articles.chicagotribune.com/1997-03-31/news/9703310046_1_wiretaps-pension-fund-teamsters-union

Rhodes, Steve. "The Lost Don." *Chicago Magazine,* October, 2005.
http://www.chicagomag.com/Chicago-Magazine/October-2005/The-Lost-Don/

"Rosemont Mayor Returns Mob-Linked Funds." *Better Government Association*, 2008.
http://www.bettergov.org/bga_in_news_20081206_01.aspx
"Rosemont Mayor Shifts Stand." *Chicago Tribune*, December 23, 2001.
http://articles.chicagotribune.com/2001-12-23/news/0112230049_1_insurance-scheme-federal-grand-jury-ties
Smith, Bryan. "In The Name of the Father." *Chicago Magazine*, May 2009. http://www.chicagomag.com/Chicago-Magazine/May-2009/In-the-Name-of-the-Father/
Smith, Sandy. "The Mob. Eavesdropped Conversations." *Life Magazine*, May, 1969.

"The Clown's Ruthless Rise." *The Chicago Sun Times*, 2007.
http://www.suntimes.com/news/mob/421215,CST-NWS-mob10.stng
"The Rest is Silence." *Time Magazine*, December 24, 1965.
http://www.time.com/time/magazine/article/0,9171,834842,00.html
Tuohy, William, John. "The Rosemont Two Step." *American Mafia*, September 2002.
http://www.americanmafia.com/Feature_Articles_233.html
Warmbir, Steve. "Son Wants Justice in '74 Death." *Chicago Sun Times*, June 11, 2007.
—. "Widow Takes on Mobsters." *Chicago Sun Times*, June 29, 2007.
—. "No Tears for Clown." *Chicago Sun Times*, February 3, 2009.
—. "The Letter that Started it All." Chicago Sun Times, August 23, 2007.
http://blogs.suntimes.com/mob/2007/08/the_letter_that_started_it_all.html#more

Websites

Dollar Times
  http://www.dollartimes.com/calculators/inflation.htm
High Beam Research
  http://www.highbeam.com/
IMDB
  Casino http://www.imdb.com/title/tt0112641/
  Goodfellas http://www.imdb.com/title/tt0099685/
John J. Flood Blog
  http://www.johnfloodblog.com/
La Cosa Nostra Database
  http://www.lacndb.com/
Organized Crime and Political Corruption
  http://www.ipsn.org/
The Chicago Sun Times
  http://www.suntimes.com/
The Chicago Syndicate
  http://www.thechicagosyndicate.com/
The Chicago Tribune
  http://articles.chicagotribune.com/
The Farmer's Almanac (Friday, September 27, 1974)
  http://www.almanac.com/
The FBI Electronic Reading Room
  http://www.fbi.gov/foia/electronic-reading-room/electronic-reading-room
The United States Attorney's Office, Northern District of Illinois
  http://www.justice.gov/usao/iln/hot/familySecrets.html
The United States Department of Justice
  http://www.justice.gov/
The United States Department of Labor
  http://www.dol.gov/compliance/laws/comp-lmrda.htm
The Wall Street Journal Archives
  http://pqasb.pqarchiver.com/wsj/advancedsearch.html

ABOUT THE AUTHOR

Matthias McCarn is a professional writer and consultant. He holds a B.A. and M.A. in English from DePaul University and is certified by the University of Chicago as an editor.

CPSIA information can be obtained
at www.ICGtesting.com
Printed in the USA
FFHW021252101218
49832240-54361FF